BEN ASHENDEN & ALEX OWEN

Ben and Alex have recorded four series of their show *The Pin* for BBC Radio 4.

They have also created an original programme for Audible, *The Special Relationship*, and an animated series for BBC 3, *Oi, Leonardo!*

Ben Ashenden & Alex Owen

THE
COMEBACK

NICK HERN BOOKS

London

www.nickhernbooks.co.uk

A Nick Hern Book

The Comeback first published in Great Britain in 2020 as a paperback original by Nick Hern Books Limited, The Glasshouse, 49a Goldhawk Road, London W12 8QP

The Comeback copyright © 2020 Ben Ashenden and Alex Owen

Ben Ashenden and Alex Owen have asserted their moral right to be identified as the authors of this work

Cover image: Feast Creative

Designed and typeset by Nick Hern Books, London
Printed in the UK by Mimeo Ltd, Huntingdon, Cambridgeshire PE29 6XX

A CIP catalogue record for this book is available from the British Library

ISBN 978 1 84842 992 5

CAUTION　All rights whatsoever in this play are strictly reserved. Requests to reproduce the text in whole or in part should be addressed to the publisher.

Amateur Performing Rights　Applications for performance, including readings and excerpts, by amateurs throughout the world (excluding the United States of America and Canada) should be addressed to the Performing Rights Manager, Nick Hern Books, The Glasshouse, 49a Goldhawk Road, London W12 8QP, *tel* +44 (0)20 8749 4953, *email* rights@nickhernbooks.co.uk, except as follows:

Australia: ORiGiN Theatrical, Level 1, 213 Clarence Street, Sydney NSW 2000, *tel* +61 (2) 8514 5201, *email* enquiries@originmusic.com.au, *web* www.origintheatrical.com.au

New Zealand: Play Bureau, PO Box 9013, St Clair, Dunedin 9047, *tel* (3) 455 9959, *email* info@playbureau.com

Professional Performing Rights　Applications for performance by professionals in any medium and in any language throughout the world (and by amateur and stock companies in the United States of America and Canada) should be addressed to Hamilton Hodell, 20 Golden Square, London W1F 9JL, *tel* +44 (0) 20 7636 1221, *email* info@hamiltonhodell.co.uk

No performance of any kind may be given unless a licence has been obtained. Applications should be made before rehearsals begin. Publication of this play does not necessarily indicate its availability for amateur performance.

The Comeback was developed by Sonia Friedman Productions and first performed at the Noël Coward Theatre, London, on 8 December 2020, with the following cast:

BEN/SID	Ben Ashenden
ALEX/JIMMY	Alex Owen
BEN/SID DOUBLE	Alex Mackeith
ALEX/JIMMY DOUBLE	Barney Fishwick
COSTA	Barney Fishwick/Alex Mackeith
OLD MAN	Robert Moore/Drew Paterson

Director	Emily Burns
Set and Costume Designer	Rosanna Vize
Lighting Designer	Prema Mehta
Sound Designer	Giles Thomas

It was produced in the West End by Sonia Friedman Productions and Tulchin Bartner Productions in association with Playing Field, Eilene Davidson Productions, Rupert Gavin/Mallory Factor and David Mirvish.

Thanks to Alex Aitken, Mary Ashenden, Roger Ashenden, Will Attenborough, Helen Bailey, Joe Bannister, James Bierman, Patrick Bone, Jack Bradley, Imogen Brodie, Sam Bryant, Ian Burns, Karen Burns, Rob Carter, Ben Chamberlain, Jack Chisnall, Alex Constantin, Alex Cooke, Heather Cryan, David Evans, Equity, Chris Farrar, Johnny Flynn, Sonia Friedman, Emma Hall, David Herman, Katya Herman, Susie Herman, Patricia Hodge, Iona Inglesby, Rupert Majendie, Emma-Louise Merritt, Fran Miller, David Nock, Alice Orr Ewing, Oxford House, Ella Saunders, Scott Skelton, Soho Theatre, Ryan Taylor, Spencer Tiney, The New Diorama Theatre, The Pleasance Theatre, Matt Trueman, Dominic Twose, WAC Arts, David Walliams, Jamie Wallwork, Paul Wanklin, Jake Wood, William Wood, Simon Woolley and Writers' Guild of Great Britain.

Characters

ALEX
  also plays JIMMY
BEN
  also plays SID

Plus COSTA (*the stage manager*), CELEBRITY GUEST,
BODY DOUBLES *and* OLD MAN

Notes on Performance

The doubling of Alex/Jimmy and Ben/Sid is an important aspect
of the show, and casting four actors would be inadvisable.

In the original production, the roles of Alex/Jimmy and Ben/Sid
were played by thirty-year-old men, but they could happily be
played by people of any age or gender. Applications to adjust
the characters' names or pronouns to suit the cast are welcomed
by the publishers.

The 'celebrity guest' certainly does not need to be a 'celebrity'
per se. Their role might be taken by anyone in the community
associated with performance, public speaking, or high status, or
indeed just by someone pulled up from the audience at random.

The sequence where Alex passes props to Ben from backstage
requires the assistance of stage management or the doubles
behind the curtain.

*This text went to press before the end of rehearsals and so may
differ slightly from the play as performed.*

ACT ONE

Scene One

We are onstage in the Didlington Arts Theatre. Once a handsome Victorian music hall, now a shabby D-list tour stop. A red curtain is lit by footlights. As the announcer's voice filters into the auditorium, the house lights fade, and the stage lights illuminate a narrow performance space.

ANNOUNCER (*voice-over*). Ladies and gentlemen, please welcome to the stage your warm-ups for this evening... Alex and Ben!

Two men in their thirties bound on from behind the curtain, stage-right, beaming smiles at the audience: ALEX, *an ebullient and impressionable optimist, and* BEN, *a stern and blunt misanthrope.*

BEN. Hello, everyone, hello! Thanks for coming. Before we begin I should tell you guys about a new system we are trialling tonight to stop us talking over each other, which has been a bit of a problem on tour –

ALEX. Yeah it's been a bit of an issue –

BEN. Well let me just explain the system and –

ALEX. Yeah, yeah.

BEN. It's called the conch system.

BEN pulls out a shell.

Basic rule is: when you're holding a shell you *can* speak –

ALEX pulls out his own shell.

ALEX. And when you're not, you can't.

BEN. No. Why have you got one?

ALEX. Oh, the shell guy did an incredible deal.

BEN snatches ALEX's shell away. ALEX is still all smiles to the audience.

BEN. Gimme that. The system is based on logic. I think Aristotle said if two competing forces –

ALEX pulls out yet another shell.

ALEX. It was an *unbelievable* deal –

BEN furiously snatches that away too, bristling with irritation.

BEN. Forget it. I'm going to get rid of these, and then we'll start properly.

BEN exits round the curtain, stage-right. ALEX gets a cheeky idea.

ALEX.... Ooh! Chance for a little prank: when Ben comes back on, I'll ask him if he says either or *i-ther*. And then, if he says either, I'll say, 'Ooh okay so you just say i-ther.' Hahaha! And then he'll say, 'No I just told you I say either.' And I'll say, 'That's what I'm saying, you just say i-ther,' and he'll say 'Noo...' and it'll go on and on and really wind him up!

BEN re-enters.

BEN. Okay, guys, so:

ALEX. Ben, quick question, mate. Do you say either or i-ther?

BEN.... er... I just vary between the two.

ALEX's smile fades. What now?

You okay?

ALEX gestures for BEN to carry on.

Alright, third time lucky! Welcome to the show, I'm Ben, and a bit about me: before I was a comedian I was actually a teacher, so be warned, if you don't laugh...

BEN wags a finger warningly as if to say 'you'll be in trouble'.

ALEX. He'll have to go back to that.

BEN. I'm not going back to that.

ALEX. No, sorry.

BEN. If I went back to anything it'd be my charity work. I actually volunteered for Greenpeace for the best part of last year.

ALEX. ... Christmas Day?

BEN. Best part.

ALEX. Right, yep.

BEN (*to audience*). You must be so excited, ladies and gents, to see your main act tonight, the comedy legends, Jimmy and Sid.

ALEX. And we'll be getting them on very shortly, but first, here's a sketch...

They begin the sketch: a film-noir-style private-investigator scene. The INVESTIGATOR (BEN), *mimes smoking a cigarette, and stares severely into the distance. The client,* MR BANLEY (ALEX), *shudders under the weight of his paranoia.*

MR BANLEY (ALEX). 'Please. I need to know. I've suspected her for months, and I've come to you out of desperation, so tell me... is she cheating on me?'

The INVESTIGATOR *takes a long drag on his cigarette and slowly turns, relishing his power.*

INVESTIGATOR (BEN). '...No.'

MR BANLEY. 'Oh, thank God! And you're sure?'

INVESTIGATOR. 'I'm a private investigator, Mr Banley, it's my job to be sure.'

MR BANLEY. 'Of course.'

INVESTIGATOR. 'Which is why what I've got to say next might come as quite a shock.'

MR BANLEY. 'What is it?'

The INVESTIGATOR *toys with* MR BANLEY, *enjoying a tantalising pause…*

INVESTIGATOR. 'I'm afraid, Mr Banley, that she's… your mother.'

Beat.

MR BANLEY. 'Which Mrs Banley did you investigate?'

The INVESTIGATOR *realises his mistake and the shameful hubris of it all hits him hard.*

INVESTIGATOR. '…I've wasted a great deal of our time.'

The sketch is over. ALEX *and* BEN *turn out to the audience.*

ALEX *and* BEN. Thank you, thank you!

ALEX. There's actually a funny backstory to that sketch, cos amazingly we saw that play out in real life!

BEN. Literally word for word, we didn't have to change anything.

ALEX. Yeah, we were watching, cracking up, and just immediately went, 'Well *that's* going straight in the act!'

BEN. It was, what, last year?

ALEX. Yeah we saw it happen in a, er… sketch show.

BEN. So big thanks to *The League of Gentlemen*. (*Seems to get distracted.*) Alex, I like your shoes by the way.

ALEX. Thanks. There's actually a funny backstory about these shoes. I got them… from a *mysterious Arab boy…*

Beguiling exotic music plays as the boys theatrically swap sides in preparation for a new scene. The music finishes.

BEN (*not going into a scene*). Well they're very nice.

ALEX. Thank you.

BEN. In this next sketch Alex plays a character called Martin… which becomes apparent almost immediately.

They begin the sketch: GAV (BEN) *and* MARTIN (ALEX) *stand beside each other, awkwardly.*

GAV (BEN). 'Martin, can I – '

BEN *nods to the audience: the 'Martin' information really does come very quickly. He returns to the sketch...*

'Martin, can I ask you a... potentially embarrassing question?'

MARTIN (ALEX). 'Sure, what's up?'

GAV. 'Well... it's... er... alright, I'll just say it. Basically, Martin... my wife and I would really... we would really like a threesome?'

MARTIN *is blindsided.* GAV *regrets asking.*

MARTIN. 'Er... oh.'

GAV. 'Sorry, I know that's a bit...'

MARTIN. 'A threesome. Right. So... so you want me to get *out* of the bed?'

GAV. 'We just think four *is* too many.'

MARTIN. 'Nice to meet you, Sarah – '

GAV. 'Just go.'

GAV *gestures to 'other people' who are apparently in the room with them, and* MARTIN *mimes holding sheets. We realise they're in bed.* MARTIN *'rolls' out.*

BEN. Thank you, ladies and gentleman, now –

ALEX. This next sketch is called 'The Funny King'!

ALEX *picks up a crown from behind the curtain, stage-right.* BEN *looks perturbed.*

BEN.... We're doing 'The Funny King'?

ALEX. Yeah yeah yeah!

The atmosphere shifts. The act clearly isn't on train tracks.

BEN. I'm not sure that...

ALEX (*to audience*). Haha, enjoy!

BEN. Well hang on, don't I wear the crown?

ALEX. No, no, I wear the crown.

BEN. You sure?

ALEX (*to audience*). Sorry, guys, a bit of housekeeping. (*To* BEN.) Yeah I wear the crown, mate.

BEN. Okay. Maybe...

ALEX. Maybe? Definitely. Yeah, yeah for 'Funny King'. I wear the crown. Definitely. Definitely.

ALEX *is enjoying being in the right.*

BEN. Okay. Just thought it was...

ALEX. You thought...? What, sorry?

ALEX *is showing* BEN *up in front of the crowd.*

BEN. No I was just saying, I thought I wore the crown.

ALEX (*smug*). Yeah I think we all know you *thought* you wear the crown, mate. Okay, guys, 'The Funny King'.

BEN (*in character*). 'Enter! Enter!'

ALEX. 'Many thanks, Your Majesty – '

(*Drops character.*) No it *is* you.

With the sketch properly derailed, BEN *is cross, taking* ALEX *upstage briefly for a firm word.* ALEX *is apologising profusely – his Icarus wings burned to a pathetic crisp.*

Remonstrations over, ALEX *turns back to the audience with a smile.*

ALEX. Sorry, ladies and gents, from the top, 'The Funny King'!

They restart the sketch.

BEN. 'Enter, enter!'

ALEX. 'Many thanks, Your Majesty.'

BEN. '"Your Majesty"? What a funny joke from a funny, *funny King* – '

ALEX (*drops character*). So it *is* me?

BEN. I don't want to do this any more. I'm just gonna see if Jimmy and Sid are ready, can you do the 'no phones' stuff?

ALEX. Oh, really?

BEN *marches angrily around the curtain, stage-right.*

Okay, guys, before we get Jimmy and Sid on, do remember to turn your...

(*Now that* BEN*'s gone...*) Okay, perfect! This gives me a chance to fill you guys in on a little surprise I've got lined up for Ben! Bit of background: Ben's always telling me to be a better whistler. He's always saying, 'Alex you're so bad at whistling, you're such a bad whistler!' *So*, I've been on a twelve-week-long whistling course. 'Ooh, Alex?' 'Yeah?' 'Did the course improve your whistling?' 'Er lemme think about that, yeah I think a *four-grand* whistling course *tends* to improve your whistling!' So get excited, guys, Ben's gonna absolutely love this – ooh here he comes! –

ALEX *is barely able to contain his mischievous glee.* BEN *marches around the curtain, stage-right.*

BEN. Okay, everyone – (*To* ALEX.) They're all set – (*To audience.*) It's the moment you've all been waiting for –

ALEX. Ben: you know how you're always telling me to improve my whistling?

BEN (*correcting*). Your *listening*.

ALEX. Fucking hell.

ALEX *is gutted.* BEN *isn't sure what's going on, but is sure that their warm-up has finished shambolically. He puts on the bravest face he can, and wraps things up.*

BEN. Well, ladies and gents, it's the moment you've all been waiting for, please put your hands together and welcome your main act for this evening, the comedy legends...

BEN *and* ALEX. Jimmy and Sid!

The audience claps. BEN *storms off around the curtain, stage-right, followed by a sheepish* ALEX.

Scene Two

The lighting shifts and widens in scope, bringing us backstage to the green room. It's grubby and depressing, filled with the typical clutter of mugs, costume rails, shoes, crisp packets. There is a single chair and two lockers, one stage-left and one stage-right, the latter of which has a sign on it reading 'out of order'. Above that locker is a cupboard.

As the real audience's applause fades we hear it apparently continue on the backstage Tannoy. BEN enters the green room around the curtain, stage-left, looking back as if towards the stage, with a grimace. When ALEX enters he gives BEN a hopeful smile, but then sees BEN's face, and dutifully mirrors him by turning to look towards the stage too. As the applause finishes we hear, on the Tannoy, JIMMY and SID (late sixties, Lancashire) greet the audience.

JIMMY (*voice-over*). Thank you, thank you! Good evening, ladies and gentlemen, I'm Jimmy, he's Sid, and – Oh for goodness' sakes, Sid, what's that in your mouth!?

BEN sulkily turns off the Tannoy and turns to watch ALEX saunter stage-right and put the crown prop away in a large props box. ALEX turns with a smile to find BEN staring at him accusingly. ALEX tries to defuse…

ALEX. That went well!

BEN. It went okay. What was that stuff about whistling?

ALEX. As in what did the course involve or why did I bring it up?

BEN….Either.

ALEX, thrilled, doubles over in excitement at the opportunity to deliver on his 'prank'.

ALEX….Ooh, okay, so you say *i-ther* –

BEN. That was weird too.

ALEX. Right, yeah.

BEN. You can't just blurt out nonsense whenever you want.

ALEX. Could go back to the conch system?

ALEX *reveals another bloody shell.* BEN*'s seething. He snatches it away.*

BEN. Is that another shell – ?! What's wrong with you?

ALEX. Sorry, Benny, I guess I'm just a bit bored of the same old material.

BEN. That 'old material' is reliable. No one wants to see rookies doing half-baked –

They've had this conversation a thousand times.

ALEX. ' – half-baked stuff.'

BEN. Well they don't! There was a guy on the front row, barely watching.

ALEX. What! No? Whereabouts?

BEN. Well –

ALEX *turns to face the stage-right wall.*

ALEX. Like if the audience was here, which one was he?

BEN. Well actually it's hard for me to visualise, let's say the audience was here…

BEN *turns to face the 'fourth wall', i.e. the real audience.*

ALEX. Can do, can do.

BEN. He was sat about… *here.*

BEN *points clearly to an audience member on the front row.*

ALEX. What was he wearing?

BEN. Um… (*Throws a surreptitious glance directly at the audience member.*) Let me go check. (*Runs to stage-left of the curtain to look 'onstage'.*) It's like he's been given a voucher for River Island for like five pounds, and he thought... 'Oh, perfect, I'll bin that.' And then in the bin he found some clothes to wear.

ALEX. Oh *him*!

BEN. Proper nutcase, did you notice he did this thing where every time I crossed my arms, he shouted at the top of his voice in this accent that – well I don't think it *was* racist – but this sort of Italian voice – he shouted, 'Oh Mama, that's one sexy pizza!'

ALEX. I did not notice that.

BEN. *Every time* I crossed my arms...

BEN looks like he's about to cross his arms... but doesn't. A pause. Then he does cross them. If the audience member doesn't play ball, he cajoles them further: 'It took him a while, but he did *do it...' After the audience member shouts the pizza line –*

ALEX. Oh yeah!

BEN. He's still doing it now!

They rush upstage to look around the curtain.

ALEX. Well, considering we had a nutcase on the front row, I think we did alright!

BEN. We're trying to make a breakthrough in this business. Not 'do alright'. (*Sulkily picks up a newspaper.*) Here we go, our latest review. This'll be a car crash...

ALEX. Not necessarily!

BEN (*reading*). 'Jimmy and Sid with support act Alex and Ben at the Didlington Arts Theatre. Those of us with long enough memories might recall Jimmy and Sid's brief heyday in 1970s light entertainment. Well now they're back on tour with a brand-new show! Expect classic end-of-the-pier humour, with visual gags, innuendo, and something for everyone, whether you're seventy or twenty. (*Turns page.*) Years older than that.'

ALEX. Well they're having a pop at Jimmy and Sid there!

BEN. 'And if they don't sound like your thing, why not just go see Alex and Ben?'

ALEX. 'Why not?' Lovely!

BEN. 'Well there are several reasons.'

ALEX. Oh, okay...

BEN. 'The writing is bad, the perfor– '

BEN *forcefully gives* ALEX *the newspaper.*

ALEX. Alright, alright.

BEN. Look, I don't *love* to say this but maybe the breakthrough just isn't going to happen.

ALEX *has heard this before. He breezily sits down on the props box and starts flicking through the paper.*

ALEX. Come on, we'll get better!

BEN. It's too late for that. Look at Jimmy and Sid: when *they* were thirty, the whole nation was watching their Christmas special. Our most recent achievement was getting down to the last five for a Bonjela ad.

ALEX. We shouldn't compare ourselves with two old-timers.

BEN *gestures to a hatstand, on which sit two of* JIMMY *and* SID*'s tophats: lurid blue, glittery monstrosities.*

BEN. No, they're crap *now* – look at their hats, they're as naff as it gets. But they were loved, they were *heroes*.

ALEX. We'll get there.

BEN. Yeah? From this dead-end dump?

ALEX. Didlington's alright! It's got a Costa.

BEN.... The stage manager?

ALEX. He's a lovely bloke. And you never know who could be out there.

BEN. I know who's out there! Pizza enthusiasts and zombies! There's another bloke on the front row who looks like he's recently been exhumed.

ALEX. No there's not a bloke who – (*Glances out at the real audience, apparently spots said bloke, becomes chastened.*) And so what if there is? There's an article here about a *Hollywood director* visiting Didlington!

BEN. No way.

ALEX (*reads*). 'Celebrated director Clint MacKay has chosen Didlington as the location for his new film. The Oscar winner said the town was perfect – ' his word, Benny, 'perfect'! (*Carries on reading.*) '– for his story about a dead-end dump. A backwater where – ' (*Stops reading.*) Oh right.

BEN. I don't know why we're doing this.

ALEX. Look, the tour's only four more weeks –

BEN. No, I mean *this*. Any of this. I think I've had enough.

ALEX *looks surprised. He's used to these post-show strops, but he hasn't heard* BEN *this defeated before. He tries to rally him.*

ALEX (*little scoff*). Come on, what else would we do?

BEN. Well I could go back to my job in the forces.

ALEX.... Your internship with Parcelforce?

BEN. My job in the *forces*, yeah.

ALEX (*backing down*). The forces, right. (*Then, jokily.*) But if you went back to that – who would I even hang out with?

BEN. Your mate Graham?

ALEX. Well... he's more your mate.

ALEX *is quibbling.*

BEN. You are friends with him?

ALEX. Er... yeah. Yeah, we get on but –

BEN. But what?

ALEX. Well no… just that he's… sorry, you said he's 'my mate', but I guess I think of him as more your –

BEN. What because I knew Graham first?

ALEX. Well yeah.

BEN. But then introduced him to you and now you *are* mates?

ALEX. Yeah, yes. Sorry. I suppose I just –

BEN *can't believe they're talking about* this.

BEN. What's the problem?

ALEX. Nothing, no, just that… you said Graham's '*my* mate', but I think of him as… (*Beat.*) Just cos he's your dad?

BEN.… Alright, fine. 'My dad.' If we stopped gigging… you could hang out with 'my dad'.

ALEX *senses something. This might be new territory.*

ALEX. Are we seriously talking about this?

BEN. I dunno, I just –

ALEX. I'm here because I love 'Alex and Ben'! We've got a future together!

BEN. We're stuck in a ghost town, bungling an act that's meant to be bulletproof, safe as houses!

ALEX *lays his cards on the table.*

ALEX. Maybe trying to be *safe* is the problem! When you said 'let's go on tour as warm-ups' I thought… I thought 'brilliant' – last few years we've been drilling our set to death, but this'll be an old 'Jimmy and Sid' audience, we can muck about, have a laugh!

BEN. Why have we been drilling it? Because we only moved on from open mics above pubs when we actually started rehearsing.

ALEX. Yeah, but then you got so obsessed with being perfect that we squeezed the life out of it.

BEN. If our *Late & Loud* audition had been perfect we wouldn't be sitting here.

ALEX. We didn't get that because we weren't enjoying ourselves, and they could tell.

BEN. Fine, let's work on that. Let's work on *enjoying ourselves*.

ALEX. No, Ben, you don't work on that, you just try stuff, wing it!

BEN. It's amateur.

ALEX. It's fun!

BEN. Oh why didn't we say that to our landlord? 'Sorry we can't pay the rent, but *we do have fun*.'

ALEX. Do you not think we did?

A taut pause. Despite himself, BEN *does kind of agree.*

BEN. So what, we should just go on and chuck some shells around?

ALEX. No, proper material! There's a whole load of stuff in here you've never let us try onstage.

ALEX *opens the props box. He takes out a sign that reads 'Free Massage!'*

What about this?

ALEX *jumps into character as if soliciting people in the street.*

'Free massage? Sir, madam? Free massage? Yeah? Great! So...'

ALEX *turns the sign around. It's a mugshot of a convict.*

'Victor Massage is innocent and *must* be set free.'

ALEX *looks to* BEN *hopefully, but* BEN *doesn't react.* ALEX *returns the sign to the box. He pulls out a piece of plain A4 card.*

Or what about this?

(*Into 'showman' character.*) 'How many times, ladies and gentlemen, do you think it's possible to fold a normal piece of card? Haha, *well...* (*Goes as if to fold, but then...*) Eight, it says here.'

He spins the card round: a big '8'.

ALEX *again looks hopefully to* BEN. *But again,* BEN*'s impassive.* ALEX *returns the card to the box. He takes out a walking cane and gasps with excitement.*

Ahhh, Benny! What about *this*!? Let's do it quickly now?... Please?... Oh come on, just really quickly.

BEN *resents being put on the spot. But looking at the cane triggers something in him, and his eyes lighten.*

BEN.... It needs the music.

ALEX. I've still got it on my phone!

ALEX *whips his phone out, places it on the props box, and hits 'play'. A grand strings arrangement floats out of the tinny speaker.* BEN*'s hand is literally forced as* ALEX *hoists him up.*

Come on!

BEN. Alright, alright.

ALEX. Let's start from here, behind here!

ALEX *leads offstage-left, for their 'entrance'. Over the strings arrangement, an announcement:*

ANNOUNCER (*voice-over*). 'Ladies and gentlemen: the winner of the lifetime achievement award... Mr Robert Greeves.'

ALEX *enters, in character as a very old man with a cane. He's walking slowly and statesmanlike, throwing warm appreciative smiles to the 'audience'.* BEN *plays an aide, walking alongside with a strong supporting arm. They eventually reach the end of the room... at which point* ALEX *continues to walk off and* BEN *turns, as if to the audience. The old man is revealed to be a bizarre red herring.*

BEN. 'What an honour, thank you so much for this award.'

ALEX *howls with laughter. Despite himself,* BEN *chuckles.*

I'm pretty sure we *did* try that once and it didn't land.

ALEX *puts the cane back into the props box.*

ALEX. Yeah, but only because someone in the audience shouted out, 'Well hang on, who was the other guy?'

BEN. Ha oh yeah!

BEN *catches himself in a good mood and puts on the handbrake. He's meant to be the serious one here.*

There you are, see: stick to what you know works.

ALEX. Well come on, that was at The Giggle Factory, what do you expect?

BEN (*that crap old place*). Oh *God*, The Giggle Factory...

ALEX. Back when I was doing that gag: 'The most embarrassing thing that's ever happened to me? Probably when I walked in on my dad wanking... I should definitely have pulled my trousers up before going in.'

BEN. That's what *I* changed it to. Before I got involved you just said, 'I once wanked in front of my dad.'

ALEX. You improved it, yeah: we were a good team! Remember at The Giggle Factory they had that slug infestation in the dressing room, but we didn't know, so when the manager came in saying 'and this is where the slugs are', we thought he meant us!

BEN. I think they had a *rat* infestation.

ALEX. Oh so he *was* talking about us?

BEN. I think so.

ALEX. Oh, bloody hell.

Their dingy past makes BEN *wrestle with both fond nostalgia and disgust.*

BEN. Why on earth did we do those gigs?

ALEX. Because we loved it! We used to come offstage absolutely buzzing in those days. You'd be laughing your head off, I'd be doing that little dance...

BEN. People would be telling you to chill out!

The nostalgia seems to be winning.

ALEX. I'd towel myself down, then we'd crack open some beers, do our secret handshake...

BEN. God, yeah.

ALEX. And then the guy in the waistcoat would come backstage and feed us fruit.

BEN. Yeah – (*Beat.*) What?

ALEX. In the old days, you know, how giddy we'd be.

BEN (*maybe I misheard*). Right, yeah.

ALEX *leaps to his feet.*

ALEX. We wouldn't come offstage sulking and bickering about the act!

BEN. No, no.

ALEX. We'd be bouncing around!

BEN (*smiling*). You more than me!

ALEX. Doing this... (*Taps heels mid-air.*)

BEN. Idiot!

ALEX. We'd talk over all the new stuff that went well.

BEN (*imagine that*). Actually *laugh* about the stuff that bombed.

ALEX. And then that old bloke in the waistcoat would come in and feed us fruit.

BEN clocks this. He didn't mishear. The momentum of the bonhomie stalls.

BEN. Sorry, what are you –

ALEX. Just saying how pumped up we were back then!

BEN. Sure, but –

ALEX. Like how we'd immediately start coming up with new bits for the next show!

BEN. Yeah...

ALEX. Then I'd towel myself down, we'd open some beers, and do the little handshake.

BEN.... Right, fine.

ALEX. And *then* the old guy in the waistcoat would pop in with, well, just a punnet of whatever was fresh –

BEN. Alex. I have *no idea* what you're talking about.

A tense silence hangs in the air.

The fruit guy wore a *tail*-coat.

ALEX. Tailcoat! That's it, yeah. What did I say?

BEN. 'Waistcoat.'

ALEX. Waistcoat, no! It was a long flowing thing! Ha, you must have thought I was going mad there?!

BEN. I did a bit, I was like, 'What's he on about!?'

ALEX / BEN. Haha! / Gawwd.

The tension has evaporated. They are shoulder to shoulder, laughing. A moment of genuine togetherness.

BEN. See, that all seems so long ago now.

ALEX. Well yeah, we did The Giggle Factory back in –

BEN. No, that… that feeling.

ALEX. Well let's get back to it. If there's a chance in hell of us making a breakthrough, we have to be the real Alex and Ben.

ALEX*'s argument has come together, and he looks at* BEN *with confidence and conviction.* BEN *still holds the power, but he's wavering. He looks at his friend. Then at the box of props…*

BEN. What else is in there?

ALEX *grins.*

ALEX. Sherlock sketch, 'Trenches'. Ooh! We could give the restaurant sketch a go?

BEN. We haven't got the props.

ALEX. Slash I've already bought them.

ALEX *produces an enormous fisherman's net from the box.*

BEN. What's this?

ALEX. The chef's hairnet.

BEN. Got a head the size of a lorry, has he?

ALEX. What's the prob?

BEN. Way too big. Mental.

ALEX. Well, no, cos sometimes props do look a lot smaller onstage.

BEN. What!? If that's the size of the hairnet then for the toothpick we'd need –

ALEX. Whoopsie daisy.

ALEX *produces a javelin.*

BEN. No way. Forget it.

ALEX *puts the javelin back and produces some darts.*

ALEX. What about the darts sketch!?

BEN*'s up for it.*

BEN. Yeah! Yeah that could be good.

ALEX. You be the landlord and I'll be the –

He walks to the middle of the room, faces the stage-right wall, and shapes to throw.

...Hang on, where's the dartboard gone?

BEN. Oh sorry, I moved it to this wall.

BEN *indicates the downstage 'fourth wall'. He's pointing right at the audience.*

ALEX. Oh nice.

ALEX *turns, ready to throw a dart at them.*

BEN. Yeah cos we were *battering* that wall.

ALEX *stops to look at* BEN.

ALEX. Well I'm throwing them so hard at the moment, it's my new technique.

BEN. What's this?

ALEX. Well you know how most pros throw like this, from the elbow?

BEN. For control?

ALEX. Exactly, and that is good for control, but if, for whatever reason, all you cared about was *sheer power*...

ALEX *takes a position that implies he's going to put all his might into hurling the dart at the audience. He stops.*

Also, little tip: hold all three like this.

He clumps all three darts in one hand.

BEN. And that's for – ?

ALEX. Surface area. Spread.

BEN (*indicates the entire width of the audience*). So
everything's in play.

ALEX. Exactly. I've sharpened them too.

BEN. So they're *lethal*?

ALEX. Yeah, got myself this darts-sharpening knife.

ALEX *produces a knife.*

BEN (*pointing upstage-right*). Whoa, do you mind putting that
in the kitchen? (*Deep, smug exhalation.*) Seeing a blade
brings back bad memories from my time in the Feds.

ALEX *recognises another slice of* BEN*'s self-mythology.*

ALEX.... Working for Fedex?

BEN (*annoyed*). My time in the Feds, yes!

ALEX (*sceptical*). Do you get trouble working as a courier?

BEN. Why else would I have a Taser in my car?

(*As a frightened customer.*) 'Oooh, that package isn't for me,
I'm not signing for that – '

(*As himself, miming Tasering.*) 'You bloody are.'

ALEX *exits, stage-right, and puts the knife away in the
unseen kitchen. He reappears with a rubber cricket ball and
a baking tray, and takes a big swing with the tray as if it's a
cricket bat.*

ALEX. Ooh another candidate! Yes, mate, 'Come on!' Haha!

BEN. We're not doing the cricket sketch – you're terrible.

ALEX. I've been practising! Check it out.

ALEX *throws the ball against the stage-right wall and hits it
on return with the baking tray.*

'COME ON!' Been using all the walls...

*He turns to the front 'fourth wall' and throws the ball out
into the crowd. Depending on whether, and how quickly,*

someone in the audience responds, ALEX *improvises. Most often, after a pause, someone throws it back.*

ALEX (*points stage-right*)....I prefer *that* wall, cos there's a bit of a delay on this one.

BEN. Bit of give, yeah. Well you'd need to buy a proper bat.

ALEX. Can't really afford one after the whistling course.

BEN. Alright then, let's hear this whistling.

ALEX. You know what, I actually still can't do it.

BEN. What kind of instructor was running this – ?

ALEX. Ooh there we go, Benny!

BEN. What?

ALEX. Our instructor sketch, 'The Swimming Instructor'!

BEN. Oh yeah...!

BEN *rifles through the box and finds two scripts.*

ALEX. It's great, why don't we try that?

BEN. Nice, just remember: this sketch has that really big twist.

ALEX. Oh yeah, it's such a funny twist.

BEN. So just really sell that moment.

ALEX. Big delivery on the twist, okay, here we go!

They get in position to rehearse.

BEN. God, when did we last rehearse new stuff?

ALEX (*immediately*). Eighty-two weeks and four days ago.

BEN *nods his acknowledgement that* ALEX *has been keeping count. They start reading.*

NIALL (ALEX). 'Hello, mate, you here for the swimming lesson?'

LIAM (BEN). 'Yeah that's me.'

NIALL. 'Sweet, I'm Niall and I'm your teacher.'

LIAM. 'Great. Are we in lane three?'

NIALL. 'The lesson… (*Big punchline.*) is in lane five!!'

This is clearly wrong, as BEN *has dropped character.*

BEN. Alex, that's not the twist.

ALEX. Is it not?

BEN. No. That the lesson's 'in lane five'?

ALEX.… Bit of a twist for the swimmer?

BEN. Well it's new information but –

ALEX (*laughing*). *Yeah!* Hahahah! Imagine if he *had* dived into lane three! The *incorrect lane!*

BEN (*let's go again*). Don't emphasise that line.

ALEX. Oh okay. *Underplay* the lane twist?

BEN. Yeah – no, that's not the twist!

ALEX. Ah –

BEN. Look further down the page, you'll see a –

ALEX. There we go! Got it. Sorry! Sorry, I'm with you now.

BEN. Okay.

Back into the sketch.

NIALL. 'Hello, mate, you here for the swimming lesson?'

LIAM. 'Yeah that's me.'

NIALL. 'Sweet. I'm Niall and I'm… (*HUGE delivery.*) your teacher!!!'

BEN *breaks character in despair.*

BEN. No!

ALEX. Panicked. I've got it now, one more time, I promise.

NIALL. 'Hello, mate, you here for the swimming lesson?'

LIAM. 'Yeah that's me.'

NIALL. 'Sweet, I'm Niall and I'm your teacher.'

LIAM. 'Great. Are we in lane three?'

NIALL. 'The lesson is in lane five.'

LIAM. 'Have you got any spare goggles?'

NIALL. 'I don't. I tend not to use them myself as I'm a ghost, but you can borrow… (*Biggest delivery imaginable.*) FROM RECEPTION!!!!'

BEN*'s head drops as soon as he hears* ALEX *gloss over the word 'ghost'. He stares at his feet.*

ALEX. Hahaha. They keep a stock of spares! Haha.

BEN…. 'Ghost' was the twist.

ALEX. Oh yeah. Gawd, how's he gonna conduct a swimming lesson if he's a ghost!? –

BEN. That's the whole point of the sketch.

ALEX. Is it?

BEN. You wrote it!

ALEX. Proud of it. Cos it's gag after gag! You've got 'wrong lane', you've got –

BEN. No, there's winging it, and then there's completely misunderstanding the material. Are you serious about this? Do you even want to do new stuff?

ALEX. Yes!! Sorry, Benny, how about something easier? Let's give this a read.

ALEX *grabs another pair of scripts and hands one to* BEN.

BEN (*remembering this one*). Right. Yes. Yeah this could be good, I'll be the guy coming in.

ALEX. Sweet.

They begin the sketch.

BEN *mimes rushing through a shop door, urgently needing a pee.*

CUSTOMER (BEN). 'Hey, where's your loo?'

MANAGER (ALEX). 'Ah, sorry, sir, the toilets are only for paying customers.'

CUSTOMER. 'Please, I'm desperate.'

MANAGER. 'I'm afraid it's a strict policy. You will have to get something.'

CUSTOMER. 'Er... okay... fine, just do me a Celtic symbol, but *quick*.'

BEN *rolls up his left sleeve and* ALEX *mimes the action and noise of a tattoo gun.*

The sketch is over and they're both cautiously happy. Maybe new stuff really will work...

ALEX. Haha yeah, that's great!

BEN. Yeah... yeah maybe we could close with that, and –

The Tannoy crackles into life again.

STAGE MANAGER (*voice-over*). Front-of-house team, that's the interval for the Jimmy and Sid show, we are clear for the interval.

ALEX. Ooh gawd, here they come. Man, my awkward greetings with Sid are getting so bad now I'm having to just avoid him. Like before the show tonight, I saw him coming down the corridor, and I just couldn't face it, so I called up my mum and asked for sex advice.

BEN.... Wasn't *that* quite awkward?

ALEX. Not as bad as saying hi to Sid. (*Peering back into the props box.*) So what next...?

BEN. Well, actually, as Costa's free, I might go tell him that tomorrow... (*The words feel strange to him.*) we'll be doing a new set.

Pause. A beam creeps across ALEX's *face as he lets this sink in. He is thrilled.*

ALEX. Okay… great!

ALEX *watches* BEN *as he walks to leave. He knows that* BEN *hasn't taken this route lightly – that deep down he's still scared.*

Benny… this will be really good for us.

BEN *wants to believe* ALEX. *But he also knows this might be their last throw of the dice.*

BEN. I hope so.

ALEX. Hey. If I was the guy in the tailcoat, I'd be gearing up to *ram* a mango down your throat.

BEN *smiles and he means it. Then he puts his serious face back on, and nods to the scripts.*

BEN. Practise!

BEN *exits around the curtain, stage-left.* ALEX *watches to make sure he's gone, then quickly takes three more shells out from under his shirt and chucks them in the props box.*

SID *enters, wearing a red sequinned top hat and a red sequinned jacket, and holding a mug. He's sweet, easy-going, and crucially, played by the actor who plays* BEN. *He's clearly frail, but still full of beans, in the way you'd imagine* ALEX *will be one day.*

ALEX (*grimacing*). Oh, hello, Sid.

SID. Hello, lad.

The greeting is immediately painfully awkward.

SID / ALEX. How are – Sorry. / Are you – Sorry.

SID *offers his right hand to shake with* ALEX.

SID. How are you!?

ALEX *approaches to take it, but* SID *has the mug in his right hand.*

ALEX. I'm very well thank – oh, sorry.

SID / ALEX. Y'hands full yes – / Can't actually. One sec. If I – swap to the other hand.

ALEX *is suggesting that he swap the tattoo shop script from his left to his right hand to enable him to shake* SID*'s free left hand with his left hand, but* SID *thinks* ALEX *is suggesting that he,* SID, *is the one who needs to 'swap to the other hand'.*

SID. Swap it, yeah can do.

ALEX *and* SID *both swap their items and now* ALEX *has a free left hand which he offers to* SID *to shake, but now* SID*'s left hand has the mug in it.*

ALEX / SID. Oh *you* swapped – / What's happened here?

SID. Well I'll just take a seat on –

ALEX. Let me put this away –

SID *goes to sit on the props box but* ALEX *has just then put his script back into it and rolled it away.* SID *smashes to the floor.*

ALEX. Oh sorry, Sid, let me just –

ALEX *offers his right hand to pick him up.* SID *thinks he's offering to take the mug and hands it over.*

SID. Very kind.

ALEX. This again?

ALEX *takes the mug and offers his left hand to hoist* SID *up, but* SID *thinks it's a handshake.*

SID. Yes, how are you?

ALEX *pulls* SID *to his feet and holds up the mug with his right hand.*

ALEX. Now, this is yours.

SID. Oh yes.

ALEX *tries to pass the mug to* SID *underneath their other, interlocked, arms, but* SID *has assumed he'd offer it where it was when presented* (*above*). *They realise the mistake and both alternate in their second attempt. The mug is now offered high up, and* SID, *with his hand now below and the mug close to his face, takes this as an invitation to be fed tea by* ALEX. *He starts to sip, and, to gain the right angle, stoops.* ALEX *meanwhile raises the mug in an awkward beat of compliance.* SID *furtively seeks purpose for his spare right hand and lands on grabbing* ALEX's *nearby left knee, which he shakes fraternally.*

SID. Yes, how are you!?

ALEX, *hopping on his free leg, falls back onto the props box, which begins to roll stage-left.* SID *grabs his mug and, in the momentum, slumps onto* ALEX's *knees, adding his weight to the now accelerating box.* ALEX, *now desperate to extricate himself from this nightmare, produces his phone.*

ALEX. Sorry, Sid, one sec I just need to make a, um… (*Dials and holds the phone to his ear.*) Hallo, Mum… yeah, just a couple of follow-up queries…

ALEX *exits.*

SID (*off, warmly, to* ALEX). Don't worry about me, lad. I can entertain myself just fine. Ha, I once watched eighteen hours of that *Antiques Roadshow* before I realised it were on pause!

SID *takes his jacket off and hangs it up, stage-right, then spots something on the 'fourth wall'.*

Oh! New dartboard! (*Spots the javelin.*) Oh! New dart! Here we go…

As SID *picks up the javelin and rocks back to fling it at the audience,* JIMMY *enters, wearing his own red sequinned top hat and red sequinned jacket. He's serious, bitter, and, crucially, played by the actor who plays* ALEX. *He's clearly doddery, but still full of ambition, in the way you'd imagine* BEN *will be one day. He puts a glass of water down and hangs up his jacket in the stage-left locker.* SID *spots him and lowers the javelin nervously, then tries to lighten the mood.*

Hello, Jim.

JIMMY (*with a curt nod*). Sid.

SID *puts the javelin away, then tries harder to defuse the tension.*

SID. That went well!

JIMMY. It went okay. What was that stuff at the beginning?

SID. I did it right, didn't I? (*Produces a silk gag.*) Put this in my mouth, pulled it out, and said, 'Oooh, *that's* my first joke!'

JIMMY. Gag. 'That's my first *gag*.'

SID *instantly realises his mistake.*

SID. Gag – yep. But come on, Jim, I didn't make any *other* mistakes.

JIMMY. 'Didn't make any other mistakes'!!?

JIMMY *takes out a large scroll and lets it unravel, dropping full length to the floor as if he's about to read out a list of crimes.*

You gave me this scroll for no reason! What's wrong with you?

SID. Sorry, Jim, I'm just struggling to remember all the new material.

JIMMY. That 'new material' is exciting. No one wants to see veterans doing stale old –

SID. ' – Stale old stuff.' I dunno, Jim, I thought we did alright!

JIMMY. We're trying to make a comeback in this business. Not 'do alright'. (*Gathering himself.*) At least we've got our new selfie sketch coming up: that's current, that's fresh. (*Takes out a selfie stick.*) I've got the stick, you remembered the iPhone?

SID. Got a phone, yep.

SID *takes out a fifties landline telephone.*

JIMMY.... *i*-Phone, Sid.

SID. Aye, a phone.

JIMMY. We can't do a 'selfie' with that phone, Sid!

SID. Course we can, no prob.

SID *wraps the cord of the phone around his head, takes the selfie stick from* JIMMY, *and starts tapping the floor irregularly with it. What begins as a confident showcase devolves into feeble improvisation.*

JIMMY.... Do you know what a selfie is?

SID. Not really.

JIMMY. Ridiculous, Sid. *Ridiculous*, and it's been the same all tour.

It looks like JIMMY*'s pent-up frustration might boil over into anger, but he doesn't have the energy.*

Look, I don't *love* to say this but maybe the comeback just isn't going to happen.

SID*'s heard this before.*

SID. Come on, we'll get better!

JIMMY. It's too late for that. Look at Alex and Ben: they're young, hungry to take our place.

SID. We shouldn't compare ourselves with a couple of novices.

JIMMY. No, they're crap now. Look at these shells, I mean, what the hell was that, but they've got energy, they're *trying* to make a splash.

SID. We've done all that.

JIMMY. Yeah? And what have we got to show for it?

SID. Everyone who's out there!

JIMMY. That lot? A bunch of nobodies and nutjobs!? There's a guy on the front row who keeps banging on –

SID. About pizza yes I know, he's back.

JIMMY *sits defeatedly.*

JIMMY. I don't know why we're doing this.

SID. Look, we can get another phone –

JIMMY. No I mean *this*. Any of this. I think I've had enough.

SID (*little scoff*). Come on, what else would we do?

JIMMY. Well I've had Blackburn Panto on the phone and they've offered me the title role in *Jack and the Beanstalk*.

SID. Jack?

JIMMY. The beanstalk.

SID. But you said –

JIMMY. It's in the title.

SID. Okay. But if we stopped the tour now – we've barely had the chance to catch up after all these years!

JIMMY. We've caught up loads. I know about your grandson Chris.

SID. Charlie.

JIMMY. *Charlie.*

SID. And she's my granddaughter.

JIMMY. Granddaughter, yep.

SID *senses something. This might be new territory.*

SID. Are we seriously talking about this?

JIMMY. I dunno, I just –

SID. I'm here because I love 'Jimmy and Sid'! We've got a history together!

JIMMY. We're stuck in a backwater, stumbling our way through an act that's meant to be fresh and modern!

SID lays his cards on the table.

SID. Maybe trying to be *modern* is the problem! When you said 'let's go on a comeback tour' I thought... I thought 'brilliant' – the act's been on ice for thirty years, but this'll be an old 'Jimmy and Sid' audience, we can do the classics!

JIMMY. Why has the act been on ice? Because those punks turned up with their new comedy, new hairdos, new swear words, and blew that old stuff away!

SID. Yeah, that was the fashion then, but then it was replaced by another fashion, and another –

JIMMY. Well what's the fashion now? Let's do that.

SID. No, Jim, we are who we are, end-of-the-pier, dicky bows and dancing!

JIMMY. It's stale.

SID. It's good!

JIMMY. Oh why didn't we say that when Granada cancelled us? 'Ooh sorry we're not edgy hip youngsters but *we are good*'?

SID. Do you not think we were?

A taut pause. Despite himself, JIMMY *does kind of agree.*

What about the '78 tour, eh...?

JIMMY. It's ancient history!

SID. We killed every night! I've still got the programme.

He produces it from stage-right. The bright seventies colours have been worn out from handling. This is precious. SID *reads from the back page:*

Bristol: killed, Bradford: killed, Sunderland: killed –

JIMMY. Minsk?

SID. Well that was a booking error. London Palladium...?

Hearing that word triggers something in JIMMY*, and his eyes lighten.*

JIMMY. Yeah, well... that went alright.

SID. Tore the house down. We'd do, er... well, got the running order here: start with 'Hello This Low', then 'Half-Pint Guv'nor', 'The Mirror Routine', pause for applause –

JIMMY. Booing, in Minsk.

SID. Then eventually belt out... (*Hinting at a musical opening.*) Da da da...!

SID is setting JIMMY *up to sing.* JIMMY *would rather not.* SID*'s grin broadens and he tries again, more forcefully.*

Da da da...!

JIMMY (*going through the motions*).
    'I'm Jim and I'm a ladies' man
    With jokes that you'll adore
    (*Then, with more effort.*) This lad right here's my biggest fan
    I'll let him tell you more.'

SID (*sings brassily*).
    'I'm Sid, I'm simple and aware
    It's daft to be with him
    But here is why we are a pair
    Now where shall we begin...
    When...'

SID ushers for JIMMY *to stand next to him.* JIMMY *protests weakly.*

JIMMY. Oh, Sid...

But SID *hauls* JIMMY *to his feet and gleefully continues with the song.*

SID.
    'When...'

JIMMY *reluctantly joins in.*

JIMMY *and* SID.

'When you're lonely and low
You've got nowhere you can go
Look for someone who makes life glow
Find them then you're not on your tod
You'll be two peas in a pod.'

*As they sing the chorus, they break into their old
choreography, stepping across the stage in unison with
jaunty elbows and heads cocked to the audience. It's joyful,
innocent – from another time. At one point this was what the
nation wanted and needed.*

*As they reach the end of the chorus, as if by magic, a musical
backing fades in and the lighting shifts to a brighter
performance state. JIMMY and SID's physicality changes
too: they seem sprightly, younger... we're seeing them in
their prime.*

The second verse begins.

JIMMY.

'You can face life on your own
And be a one-man band.'

JIMMY *mimes playing the piano.*

SID.

'But even virtuoso players
Need a helping hand.'

SID *mimes putting his fingers on the same keyboard.*

'When me and him – '

JIMMY.

'That's Jim and I – '

SID.

'Yes sorry me and he – '

JIMMY.

'No!'

SID.

'Now I've lost my track – '

JIMMY.

'But with a pal you're not at sea…'

JIMMY *and* SID.

'When you're lonely and low
You've got nowhere you can go
Look for someone who makes life glow
Find them then you're not on your tod
You'll be two peas in a pod.

If you feel a bit blue
Like you haven't a clue
Grab that someone who makes you *you*
No matter the hurdles and bumps
Together you'll come up trumps.'

The music keeps vamping as JIMMY *and* SID *leap into quick-fire gags with slick energy and surgical timing. It's very audience-facing, old-school, and drilled.*

SID. 'Jim, Jim, I can't find the pointing stick!'

JIMMY (*produces a large stick with a very clear arrowhead and points it towards* SID). 'Here it is Sid.'

SID (*looking to where the stick is pointing, rather than at the stick itself*). '…Where?'

JIMMY (*raising a clenched fist*). 'D'oh!!'

SID. 'Here, Jim, good news: I've invested all our money into our very own clothing line!'

JIMMY. 'Oh yes?'

SID. 'It'll stretch right across the garden.'

JIMMY. 'Oh can you do nothing right? Here, Sid, what's this?'

JIMMY *mimes 'film', then 'one word', then starts doing big crazy actions: skiing, log chopping, frying a fish.*

SID. 'Charades?'

JIMMY. 'Oh, Sidddd!'

JIMMY *and* SID (*singing*).
  'When you're lonely and low
  You've got nowhere you can go
  Look for someone who makes life glow
  Find them then you're not on your tod.'

SID.
  'Even if he's a bit odd!'

JIMMY. 'Who are you calling odd!'

JIMMY *and* SID.
  'Trust me, I swear to God!'

  *Over the course of the final lines, the musical backing
  gradually fades away again, the lighting returns to as it was,
  and* JIMMY *and* SID*'s physicality returns to normal...*

  'You'll be two peas in a pod
  You'll be two peas in a pod
  You'll be two peas in a pod!'

  They are back in the green room and the flashback is over.
  JIMMY *is quiet, but he's not looking away.* SID *takes a deep
  breath, filling himself with the memory before it evaporates
  completely.*

SID. See, Jim? Doesn't that feel right?

JIMMY. It's always felt right, Sid... but come on, we agreed:
  times had changed, we had to forget about all that.

SID. Well I haven't been able to! I thought moving to the
  cottage and pottering round the garden would help but...
  I've missed it, Jim.

  JIMMY*'s passionate, but not angry.*

JIMMY. You've missed it? Try slogging through decades of
  D-list appearances and reality telly, constantly *reminded* of
  what you've lost. I'd much rather be the one who walked
  away from showbiz, never to look back.

SID. I was *always* looking back. That's why I'm here.

JIMMY. Asking your old mate to chuck the comeback away for a nostalgia trip.

SID. Jim, if there's a chance in hell of us making a comeback, we have to be the *real* Jimmy and Sid.

SID's argument has come together, and he looks at JIMMY *with confidence and conviction.* JIMMY *still holds the power, but he's wavering. He drops his head. Deep down he agrees, and always has done.*

JIMMY. Okay… *maybe* you're right but, come on, Sid: what good would it do impressing the king-makers of Didlington?

SID. You never know who could be out there, this is where Pat Digby comes to scout new acts!

JIMMY. Pat died twenty years ago.

SID. Okay… well he's not looking anywhere *else* then, is he?

JIMMY. Give over, Sid.

SID. No, come on: who's in tonight? Let me get the ticket list – prepare to be amazed. (*Fetches clipboard.*) We have in tonight… '*Patricia Longworth…*' oooh!

JIMMY. Who's that?

SID. Don't know, 'oooh', *mystery*, exciting! Next up: 'Billy Roper', he might be a producer.

JIMMY (*looking over* JIMMY*'s shoulder*). Says 'child's ticket'.

SID. Okay not him, but hang on 'Christian DiMaggio' – now that's a classy name, that's a power player –

JIMMY. What seat's he on?

SID. A7.

JIMMY. That's just the pizza nutcase.

SID. Alright, who else we got? 'Clint MacKay', suppose he's the theatre handyman, is he?

JIMMY *stops in his tracks.*

JIMMY. Clint MacKay? You're joking.

SID. What?

JIMMY. Well he's that director, int' he?

SID. What you on about?

JIMMY. The Hollywood bloke who's making his film here!

SID. What, you mean this is –

JIMMY (*taking the clipboard*). – Clint MacKay!! Oh my God!
No, must be someone with the same name, it can't be *actual*
Clint MacK–

SID. It'd explain the Ferrari outside?

JIMMY. A Ferrari, in Didlington?

SID. Take a look.

*JIMMY gives SID the ticket list back and, with a little help,
climbs onto the stage-left chair to get a view through an
unseen high-up window.*

JIMMY. No you're messing – you're out to have me break my
neck on a wild goose chase, looking for a car that's never in
a million years going to be – (*Reaches full height and can
now see through the window.*) *What* a vehicle!

SID. 'Clint MacKay...' well there you go, Jim, there's our
king-maker!

They're like children on Christmas morning.

JIMMY. ...we need to put on a show!

SID. Just a bit!

JIMMY. God, this is big-time. This is it!

SID (*poking fun*). You still wanna do the selfie sketch?

JIMMY. We're not doing the selfie shit, we'll do the old
favourites!

SID. Here. We. *Go!*

*SID runs, stage-left, to pin up the '78 programme, with its
faded setlist proudly on show.*

JIMMY. 'Mirror Routine': can you remember it?

SID. How could I forget?

JIMMY (*getting ready to rehearse*). From the top then? Bloody hell! When was the last time we did the old act?

SID (*immediately*). Thirty-two years and four months ago.

JIMMY nods acknowledgement that SID has been keeping count, and they start the rehearsal. The routine is that JIMMY plays a man going to check himself in the mirror, and SID plays his reflection, copying every movement.

JIMMY (*calling off*). 'Alright, lads, I'm coming, just going to the bog, I'll be one sec.'

JIMMY and SID turn to face each other (through 'the mirror'). JIMMY takes a big breath.

'You ready for this, top fella?'

He leans into 'the mirror' and checks his teeth. With his fingernail he picks something out and flicks it away. He leans back, claps his hands together, rubs them.

'Big night on the tiles!'

He mimes picking up cologne and spraying either side of his neck. He replaces the cologne, then pauses, thinks, and picks it up again. After a moment's hesitation he pulls the waistband of his trousers out and sprays cologne down his crotch. He replaces the cologne, turns to the side, and pulls up his shirt.

'Yeah you're looking good, lad. (*Slaps his belly.*) Lean. And. Strong!'

He faces his reflection again and does a most-muscular pose, then points at himself.

'You are on the pull tonight!'

He peers surreptitiously over his shoulder, looks back at 'the mirror', and then nervously undoes his belt and lowers his trousers. This is getting weird.

'Ooh... what you got down there?'

He grabs his crotch through his pants, and leans right into his reflection.

'NICE. BIG. PACKAGE!'

He pulls his trousers back up.

'Well good to meet you but I should go.'

SID. 'No worries, mate.'

They shake hands, destroying the mirror illusion and revealing that this was actually two separate men who have simply been behaving bizarrely.

The sketch is over. JIMMY and SID bow out to the imagined audience. SID goes beserk with laughter and even JIMMY is chuckling now.

Still got it, eh? See, *that's* what we do! Clint'll love it, he'll have his chequebook out, and then we hit him with...

They're on an absolute roll. This is feverish.

JIMMY. The Frankenstein sketch!?

SID. Perfect!

SID *produces two masks. One a grotesque Frankenstein's monster, the other a friendly mouse.*

Ooh, Jim, which mask is it again?

JIMMY. Oh stop messing, Sid!

SID. Haha, right, here we go – I'll come on from here!

SID *goes stage-right, into the kitchen.*

JIMMY. Yeah oh and, Sid? Really go for it: make a terrifying entrance.

SID (*pokes his head out*). Make a what?

JIMMY. When you come on as the monster, knock Clint's socks off, make a proper *terrifying* entrance.

SID *has a ploy here...*

SID. You want me to make a 'terrifying entrance'?

JIMMY. If that's no trouble, your bleedin' highness!

SID (*goes back into the kitchen*). Oh no, that's okay, you'll get a terrifying entrance alright...

JIMMY. Okay, here we go.

(*In Gothic character.*) 'Ladies and gentlemen, I present to you my most heinous creation yet: monster... come on!'

A long pause. Eventually SID *enters, carrying a grim and Gothic-looking prop doorway, adorned with skulls, spiders and cobwebs.*

SID. 'WARGGHH!!'

JIMMY. Missed your cue – what the *hell* is that?

SID. Well, haha, you asked me to 'make a terrifying entrance'.

JIMMY *drinks in the insanity of what's happened.*

JIMMY. For goodness' sakes, Sid, put that away and do it properly – Where did you even get the materials?

SID. Had stuff left over from making you that scroll!

JIMMY. Get back in there! Enter as soon as you hear 'come on'.

SID *returns to the kitchen.*

(*In Gothic character.*) 'Ladies and gentlemen, I present – '

(*Out of character.*) I should really direct this *at* Clint. Where's he sat...?

He peers around the curtain, stage-left, and exits to get a better look 'at the audience'. After a beat, ALEX *pops his head in.*

ALEX (*still on the phone*). Well that's certainly very graphic imagery, Mum... okay... bye-bye.

He breathes a sigh of relief that SID *is nowhere to be seen, and enters fully. Now that he has nothing to do... he picks up his baking tray and cricket ball for a bit of practice, and looks as if to throw the ball out to the same audience member as before.*

No actually, not after last time…

He bounces it off the stage-left wall instead, and hits the ball cleanly.

Yes, mate, 'COME ON!'

SID *hurtles in from the kitchen with the monster mask on (this is, in fact, a* SID BODY DOUBLE). ALEX, *terrified, swings the baking tray at him instinctively, knocking him out cold.* ALEX *throws the tray into the wings in panic, and cowers on the floor away from the body.*

FUCKING HELL, OH MY GOD, WHAT!!?? WHAT THE HELL!!??

Recovering himself, he tentatively moves over and lifts up the monster mask.

Oh no. Sid!? Sid, mate, are you okay? Sid, wake up, pal?

ALEX *taps* SID*'s face. No reaction.*

Oh my God…

The Tannoy crackles back into life.

STAGE MANAGER (*voice-over*). Beginners for the second half, this is your five-minute call, five minutes. The second act of the Jimmy and Sid show will commence in five minutes.

ALEX *is in a living hell. Now what? After some floundering, he drags* SID*'s body into the kitchen. As soon as the body has disappeared,* BEN *enters round the curtain, stage-left.*

BEN. Alex? Hey, Costa just told me that Clint MacKay's actually *in the audience tonight*, how mad is that?!

ALEX. Clint MacKay's watching *tonight*? Oh my God…

BEN. What? (*Clocks* ALEX*'s expression.*) Are you alright?

ALEX. Disaster.

BEN. What's happened?

BEN*'s instantly on edge.*

ALEX. I was practising the cricket sketch, I accidentally clocked Sid round the head, now he's out cold.

BEN. 'Out cold'!? – Where is he?

ALEX. I've stashed him in the kitchen.

BEN. You've *stashed him in the kitchen*?!?

BEN storms over to the kitchen to look, and recoils in shock.

You've stashed him in the kitchen.

ALEX. Shall I call a doctor?

BEN. We haven't got time to call a doctor, they've got to be on in four minutes!

ALEX. I'll get Jimmy.

BEN. Don't get Jimmy!! If he finds out you've sabotaged his shot at Hollywood he'll fire us, we'll be blacklisted, the end!! Jesus, Alex, just when we were feeling excited about –

ALEX (*weakly mimes batting gesture*). That's why I was working on the –

BEN. Well we're never going to perform it now. Or anything. Ever again.

A beat. ALEX *looks away in embarrassment, and notices* JIMMY *and* SID*'s blue hats…*

Maybe we *should* find Jimmy. Just get this over and done with.

ALEX. Wait a second, Benny… This might sound a bit mad but… you and Sid… do look quite similar…?

BEN…. What are you saying?

ALEX *picks up a blue hat.*

ALEX. Well… you could do the second act instead? Jimmy might not know the difference. How's your Sid impression?

BEN (*perfect* SID). 'It's actually not bad, lad.'

ALEX. *Whoa*, that is good!

BEN. Yeah, but they're doing different stuff every night, I wouldn't know the lines.

ALEX. Come on, mate, it'd be alright – !

BEN. Why am I having to – Piss off, you're the one who's knocked out a pensioner! I mean, at least if you'd *told* me you were gonna knock Sid out I might have said, 'Alright, I'll take out Jimmy as well then, we can claim they're both accidents, go on instead in front of Clint... then it'd be *our* big break...'

They let this sink in. Conspiratorial music begins.

ALEX. So... hypothetically, I mean... you said 'take out Jimmy' but I mean you wouldn't Taser him, would you?

BEN. No, no no, course not, he's an old man. No... I wouldn't need to.

ALEX *raises an eyebrow.* BEN *looks around smugly. Something massive is brewing here.*

Hypothetically... I could hypnotise him. It's called NLP, Neurolinguistic Programming. Over the last three to five years, I've – and it's *four* years – I've been unlocking the power of the brain through subliminal messaging. Trigger words, body language, miniscule suggestions so subtle my target never realises he's under my control.

ALEX. So you're saying...

BEN. I'm saying I could sleep him.

ALEX (*conscience kicking in*). But I guess... I mean, Sid was an accident, but *this* would be –

BEN. Amoral, opportunistic, completely driven by greed –

ALEX. I say we do it.

BEN. Me too. Right, get back in the kitchen.

ALEX. Okay...

ALEX *darts off into the kitchen.*

BEN. Hear any of this, it'll knock you spark out too. You can't hear me now, can you?

ALEX *pops back.*

ALEX. No, all good.

Beat. ALEX *realises the issue.*

...I'll find something to cover my –

He leaves again.

BEN. Cover your ears, yep.

BEN *rehearses his NLP trigger movements.* ALEX *returns, now with a duvet draped over his head and a pair of massive headphones on over that (this is, in fact, an* ALEX BODY DOUBLE). *He gives a thumbs-up to* BEN.

BEN. Nice one! Okay, off you go, pal.

Beat. ALEX *obviously now can't hear him.*

Alex? Off you pop, mate. Ale– Oh I see.

BEN *bundles him off into the kitchen, and as soon as he's disappeared,* JIMMY *enters around the curtain stage-left.*

JIMMY. Okay, Sid, Clint's more or less in the middle of the stalls so... (*Spots* BEN.) Oh, Ben. Have you seen where Sid went because we need to go back on for the second act.

BEN *clicks his fingers performatively, and turns to face* JIMMY. *As he does so, slick, heist-movie music kicks in.*

BEN (*with meaning*). Hello, Jimmy. Say, I was just thinking, you look good for your age, you must get a lot of beauty... (*Nods once, emphatically.*) sleep.

BEN *looks at* JIMMY *triumphantly.* JIMMY *is nonplussed. Will it work?...*

JIMMY. Er, well, thank you, yes I suppose I do.

BEN (*a tiny bit thrown*). Mmm. Listen though: a lot of beauty... *sleep.*

BEN *makes a few odd physical movements. Again – no change to* JIMMY.

JIMMY.... Yeah. Now, Ben, *do* you know where Sid is cos we've got to go on for the rest of the show.

BEN (*panicking*). Yes, what are you going to do for the *rest* of the show?

BEN *really goes for his NLP movements. He mutters the word 'rest' suggestively a few times. Nothing.*

JIMMY. Ben... are you alright?

The music cuts. Pause. BEN*'s smugness has been replaced by sheer desperation. Unsure how he can get out of this... he goes nuclear.*

BEN.... Go to sleep.

JIMMY. What?

BEN. Get the hell to sleep, man.

JIMMY (*going to the stage-left locker to get his jacket*). What on earth are you talking about? I'm trying to find my mate to go back onstage for the biggest night of our lives and you're talking nonsense about –

BEN *pushes* JIMMY *into the locker and slams the door.* JIMMY *starts to shout, so* BEN *reopens the door and punches him.* JIMMY *is silent.* BEN *shuts the door and smiles to himself. His conceit returns at full force.*

BEN. Isn't the mind amazing?

ALEX *returns.*

ALEX. Did it work?

BEN.... He's in the locker, yeah.

ALEX. Wow...

BEN. We need to put on a show!

Exciting, dramatic music fades in.

ALEX. Just a bit!

BEN. God, this is big-time. This is it!

ALEX. What are we even gonna do out there, we haven't had time to work out our new set?!

BEN. So we *properly* wing it. The real Alex and Ben!

ALEX. And if it doesn't work... our careers are over?

BEN. And *we're* over. We make the breakthrough now, or we go our separate ways. I'd go back to Parcelforce and you... well, I don't know what you'd do.

ALEX (*taking out a conch*). Try and sell some of these probably.

BEN. Is that *another shell*?!

ALEX. He was basically giving them away.

BEN. Right, I'm putting these where you can't reach them...

BEN *takes this shell, and the shell he previously chucked onto the table, and marches over to the stage-right cupboard.*

ALEX. Ooh, Benny, wait – !

BEN *reaches up to the cupboard.*

BEN. No, Alex – this is the biggest night of our lives. We can't afford any more slip-ups.

BEN *opens the cupboard, and an avalanche of hundreds of shells cascade into the room, leaving him buried under a vast pile.*

STAGE MANAGER (*voice-over*). Beginners to stage, beginners to stage, the second act is about to begin.

Blackout.

End of Act One.

ACT TWO

Scene One

The full stage lights come up. But there is an awkward pause.

A person in black we haven't seen before enters with a headset. They look a little uncomfortable as they wait for the audience to settle. What is going on?

COSTA. Hello, ladies and gentlemen, I hope you had a good interval. I'm the stage manager, my name's Costa, and I'm really sorry, but due to unforeseen circumstances, Jimmy and Sid are unable to continue for the second act of tonight's show. So instead, we're handing back to your warm-ups: please put your hands together for Alex and Ben!

COSTA *exits, whilst* ALEX *and* BEN *enter around the curtain, stage-right, with enormous enthusiasm and energy. They're ready to give this everything.* BEN *carries and places a chair (the one we saw backstage in Act One), stage-right.*

ALEX. Yes, hello, everyone, we are back!

BEN. And this first sketch is set in a swimming pool. (*Sotto, to* ALEX.) Sure you got this?

ALEX. Yeah yeah yeah.

They begin the sketch.

NIALL (ALEX). 'Alright, mate, you here for the swimming lesson?'

LIAM (BEN). 'Yep, that's me.'

NIALL (*huge punchline delivery*). 'I'm a ghost!'

The sketch is ruined. ALEX *beams, unaware.* BEN *swears hard under his breath but pivots to the audience to pretend that was its natural ending.*

BEN. Fuuck. There it is then, that's the first sketch: short and sweet, doesn't make any sense whatsoever. This next sketch is about Sherlock Holmes.

ALEX. I'll just get the props.

ALEX *exits around the curtain, stage-right.*

BEN. Sorry, everyone, obviously it's been a bit of a scramble getting this together so last-minute, Alex is just fetching –

ALEX *enters around the curtain, stage-left, into the green room. The lighting splits in two: stage-right is still lit like it's 'onstage', but stage-left is lit like it's 'green room'. We are seeing* BEN *onstage and* ALEX *backstage at the same time.*

ALEX *dashes over to the props box stage-left. He calls to* BEN *round the curtain, as if throwing his voice. When* BEN *responds, he does so by calling behind the curtain, stage-right.*

ALEX. Ben?

BEN. Yep?

ALEX. Just gonna pass the props through, for speed.

BEN. Yeah good thinking.

ALEX. So here comes the teapot...

ALEX *'passes' a teapot behind the curtain, stage-left, and* BEN *receives it, apparently magically, around the curtain, stage-right.*

BEN. Nice one.

BEN *places the teapot on the floor.*

ALEX. Now the house of cards...

ALEX *delicately picks up a quivering house of cards on a tray.*

BEN. Careful with that, took me ages to –

ALEX. Yeah yeah. Here we go... ooh!

Just as he passes the tray behind the curtain he stumbles such that BEN *'receives' a tray with the cards now collapsed, fluttering everywhere.*

BEN. This is what I'm talking about...

ALEX. Sorry! Next is the whisky bottle...

ALEX *'passes' a whisky bottle.* BEN *receives it as a miniature whisky bottle.* BEN *is perplexed. Perhaps sometimes props* do *come out smaller onstage?*

BEN. Ooh, hang on.

ALEX. What?

BEN. That actually *has* come out a bit small.

ALEX. Yeah, I told you.

BEN. Fair play.

ALEX. Okay, here's the umbrella...

ALEX *'passes' a tightly furled full-size umbrella, but* BEN *receives a tiny cocktail umbrella.*

BEN. Wow, I see what you mean.

ALEX. Shall we try the picture of Wayne?

BEN. Just out of curiosity, yeah.

ALEX *'passes' a large laminated photo of Wayne Rooney.* BEN *receives a laminated photo of rapper Lil Wayne.*

Ah no that's come out as Lil Wayne. No, no way we can use that.

BEN *passes it back but then a ball rolls out onstage by his feet.*

Ooh... okay, ha, little mistake there, we don't need this. Alex?

ALEX. Yeah?

BEN. Catch.

ALEX *readies himself for the catch and* BEN *throws the ball behind the curtain, stage-right. It appears behind the curtain, stage-left, as a huge ball which clatters into* ALEX*'s shoulder.*

ALEX. Whoa!

BEN. Ooh, that looked nasty. I've got some Deep Heat?

BEN *produces a can of Deep Heat from his back pocket.*

ALEX (*proffering his hurt shoulder*). Would you mind?

BEN *sprays behind the curtain, stage-right, and the mist appears behind the curtain, stage-left, as a huge powerful jet of smoke, pummelling* ALEX*'s face.*

AAARGH! You know what, I think I'll just pop back onstage, Benny, cos everything's getting a bit –

BEN. Weird, yep.

ALEX *exits the green room around the curtain, stage-left, and the lighting returns to the fully 'onstage' state.*

(*To the audience.*) Okay, guys, as soon as Alex returns we'll get started with…

BEN *glances behind the curtain, stage-right, as if watching* ALEX *come towards him, but* BEN*'s eyes seem to track* ALEX *getting lower and lower. He looks all the way down towards the floor, shocked.*

Oh no.

Melancholy music. It appears that ALEX *has shrunk too?!*

No… Oh my God, *oh my God…*

He bends down to pick something up from behind the curtain. He reveals it: a small blonde Action Man.

…A… Alex?… Oh no. Alex, mate? No way. ALEX!!!!

The real ALEX *appears. The music cuts.*

ALEX. What's up?

BEN. Haven't seen one of these in ages!

There was no cause for alarm in the end.

Just gonna put it backstage for safe keeping.

BEN, *carrying the Action Man, exits around the curtain, stage-right.*

ALEX. Okay, guys, sorry for the delay, we'll be ready to start the sketch any moment.

BEN *enters the green room and the lighting splits again. To* BEN*'s shock, the Action Man has become life-size.* BEN, *taken aback and straining under the weight of the model, dumps it near the stage-left table, accidentally knocking the cup of water* JIMMY *put down earlier onto his trousers.*

BEN. Oh shit!

ALEX. What's up, Benny?

BEN *looks down at his groin to see a large wet patch. He can't go back onstage like this.*

BEN. I'm gonna have to sort something, gimme a minute!

ALEX (*to audience*). Okay, looks like another little snag, er... ah! This is the perfect time for me to teach you the Sherlock *song*, which we'll be singing together later in the sketch.

ALEX *fetches a lyrics sheet ('Here comes Sherlock in his deerstalker hat!') and conductor's baton from behind the curtain, stage-right, whilst on the other side of the stage in the green room* BEN *puts the life-size Action Man behind the curtain and fetches a hairdryer.*

So, here are the lyrics, let me teach you the tune. It goes like this...

Just as ALEX *starts singing and pointing to the lyrics,* BEN *directs the hairdryer towards his damp patch and turns it on. It's very loud, drowning out* ALEX*'s performance entirely and making it impossible for the audience to hear the tune. As* ALEX *gets to the end,* BEN *turns the dryer off.*

' – haaaaat.' Okay, sing it back to me! All together on three… two… one!

ALEX *points at the words one by one and encourages the audience to sing. They make an attempt (which will, of course, be entirely discordant). BEN peers around the curtain, stage-left, as if watching the audience's surreal attempt at the song. Once they've finished, ALEX looks completely baffled…*

…Spot on! I'm really impressed with that cos it's quite an avant garde tune but you guys *nailed* it.

BEN *drops the dryer, exits the green room, and returns onstage. The lighting goes back to the fully 'onstage' state.*

BEN. Okay, we're finally ready, so please enjoy: the Sherlock sketch.

BEN *sits on the chair.*

(*As Sherlock.*) 'Ah, Dr Watson, please take a seat – '

(*Drops character.*) Sorry, Alex, I've just remembered, we need another chair, don't we?

ALEX. Ah. Sorry, guys – one more kink to iron out, I think there's another chair…

BEN. Just back there?

ALEX (*heading to the green room*). Backstage, yeah.

BEN (*to audience*). We're just gonna nip and grab another chair, guys, one sec.

ALEX *and* BEN *rush around the curtain, stage-right. They enter the green room and the lighting becomes fully 'green room'. ALEX spots the 'backstage chair', which is obviously in reality the same chair that's onstage.*

ALEX. Yeah, there it is.

BEN. Real focus now, let's show Clint what we can do!

He takes the chair around the curtain, stage-left, followed by
BEN. *They enter around the curtain, stage-right, and the*
lighting returns to fully 'onstage'.

ALEX (*placing chair for himself*). A chair for Dr Watson!
Okay, here we go, the Sherlock –

BEN. Ooh – hang about. Where's my chair gone?

They notice that the original chair BEN *sat in has*
apparently just vanished.

ALEX. Oh, what?

BEN. Did you move it?

ALEX. No I was backstage with you.

BEN. So... someone's playing silly buggers.

They look out to the audience, disapprovingly.

ALEX. Okay... looks like we got a joker in the house. Don't
take chairs, guys!

BEN. I'll go see if I can find another one.

ALEX. I'll keep watch, yeah.

BEN *rushes around the curtain, stage-right.*

Okay, guys, Benny's just fetching another chair now and
then we'll be good to go!

BEN *appears in the green room. The lighting splits.*

BEN *spots 'another chair' (the same chair again) and grabs*
it. ALEX *doesn't notice, as he's facing the audience.*

BEN (*calling to* ALEX). Found one!

BEN *exits the green room. The lighting goes back to the fully*
'onstage' state.

ALEX. Nice one, Benny! Okay, guys, Ben's got another chair
so as soon as he gets back it'll be time for the Sherlock –

BEN *returns onstage and immediately notices that 'Watson's*
chair' is now missing.

BEN. Where's *your* chair now?

ALEX. Oh *what*?

This is becoming a nightmare.

BEN. What have you done with it!?

ALEX. No, nothing, I literally turned my back for one second –

Enough. BEN *needs to keep the show on the road.*

BEN. Okay, okay, let's just do it with one chair.

ALEX. One chair. Okay – (*Cheeky, to audience.*) Not how it's written, but who cares!

BEN. 'Ah, Dr Watson, please, take a seat.'

ALEX. 'I'd rather stand Sherlock.'

BEN. 'Good man – '

ALEX (*drops character*). It's *exactly* how it's written.

BEN. Didn't even need two. On with the sketch!

(*Back into character.*) 'Good man! I like a chap who stands. As you can see, I don't even have a chair myself.'

They stop again.

ALEX. So we don't need *that* one!

BEN. I'm going mad here...

BEN *rushes around the curtain with the chair.*

ALEX. So sorry, guys, thanks for bearing with us.

BEN *enters the green room, the lighting splits, and he drops the chair off, before exiting again.*

When Ben gets back we'll crack on with, thankfully, *no chairs* –

BEN *returns onstage and the lighting returns to fully 'onstage'. He spots that the chair has apparently reappeared behind* ALEX *again! He screams.*

BEN. Where's *that* chair come from!

ALEX (*turns and sees the ghostly apparition*). ARGHHH!!!!!

BEN. Right, forget that sketch, far too stressful. 'Trenches' next? Yes, so this one actually has three characters, guys, so we will need a volunteer to join in...

(*Scans the audience... spots the 'pizza' guy.*) Erm... no don't want to hear about deep-crust, so yeah – you. You, mate, you'll do, up you come, round of applause!

BEN *ushers an apparently random audience member up onstage. They are, in fact, a* CELEBRITY GUEST (*ideally this is someone known for being a performer*).

ALEX. Hello, what's your name?

The GUEST *answers*.

BEN. Okay, and what do you do for a living?

These answers and ALEX *and* BEN's *responses to them are tweaked for whoever the* GUEST *is, but the overall sentiment is that the esteemed visitor is treated like an inexperienced, nervous interloper.*

Well this is an easy gig, you've only got one line, so you'll be okay.

ALEX. Yeah and don't be intimidated by our level cos we did go to drama school and everything, ever heard of a little place called *RADA*...?

GUEST. Yeah.

ALEX. Near there, quite near there.

BEN. So you're playing Officer Jenkins, and your line is 'Gentleman: let's show these bastards the meaning of war.' You want to give that a go?

GUEST. 'Gentleman: let's show these bastards the meaning of war.'

BEN.... Well don't worry, that was only a rehearsal. So you enter round the curtain to here. And Alex and I start the scene over here.

ALEX. And your cue to come on is –

BEN. Actually, you know what, don't worry, it's such an obvious cue you'll be fine – it's made very clear. Alright, ready? Let's do the 'Trenches' sketch.

The GUEST *exits, awaiting their entrance. Atmospheric war sounds and tense music. A loud BOOM of a distant bomb.*

BEN. 'I'm not sending ten thousand men over the top without confirmation from Officer Jenkins.'

ALEX. 'But time is of the essence! The enemy lines are – Wait! I can hear Jenkins coming now...'

The GUEST *enters.*

GUEST. 'Gentlemen: let's show these bastards the meaning of war – '

ALEX (*dropping character*). Ooh, not yet, pal.

The music cuts. This wasn't the cue. ALEX *and* BEN *are a bit put out by the mistake. The* GUEST *looks confused: they reasonably assumed that was the right moment to enter.*

BEN. Just wait for the cue if you can, yeah?

GUEST. Oh, sorry.

ALEX. No don't worry, it will be really clear.

BEN. Okay, from where we were, come on.

The GUEST *exits. The music returns as before.*

ALEX (*back in character*). ' – wait! I can hear Jenkins coming now... No... I must be imagining things.'

BEN. 'This war plays tricks with the mind.'

ALEX. 'How long will it take Jenkins to get here!?'

BEN (*checking a map*). 'Jenkins is coming from Trench D so... oh Christ, that'll take ages. Ah, thank God for that – *Jenkins is here!*'

The GUEST *enters.*

GUEST. 'Gentlemen: let's show these bastards – '

BEN / ALEX. No no no. / Not yet!

The music cuts. BEN *itches with frustration. The* GUEST *can't believe* that *wasn't the cue.*

BEN. From *our* point of view, friend, we're trying to make the second half 'actually good', so it's sort of a case of don't take the piss? Okay.

The GUEST *exits. The music returns as before.*

(*Checking a map.*) 'Ah, thank God for that – *Jenkins is here!* (*Points at map.*) In Trench B! Much closer.'

ALEX. 'We can't wait any longer. You've got three seconds to make the call. Three... two... one... and go for it now [*insert* GUEST*'s real name*]!'

The GUEST *enters.*

GUEST. 'Gentlemen – '

ALEX / BEN. NO!!!! / Not yet!!!!

The music cuts. How is that not the cue!?

ALEX. Sorry, yeah, that is quite confusing, Ben's character is also called [GUEST*'s real name*].

BEN. We'll leave it there, round of applause for [GUEST*'s real name*]!

The GUEST *is ushered back to their seat in the audience.*

Amazing what passes as talent these days. Okay, Alex, darts next?

ALEX. Great yeah, I'll go grab them!

ALEX *exits around the curtain, stage-right.*

BEN. Wicked, I'll just make some space…

> ALEX *enters the green room and the lighting splits. Onstage* BEN *clears the Sherlock props and chair to one side, whilst backstage* ALEX *goes to grab the darts, when suddenly the door of the stage-left locker rattles.* ALEX *freezes. Another rattle.* JIMMY *is waking up!* ALEX *rushes back onstage, the lighting returning to fully onstage, and he whispers frantically in* BEN's *ear.*

> (*Concerned, but saving face.*) 'Emergenc–'? One sec, everyone, let me go and talk some sense into this one. Haha.

> BEN *exits and both he and* ALEX *re-enter the green room. The lighting becomes fully 'green room'.*

> What's wrong?

> *The stage-left locker door swings open with a bang, and* BEN *instinctively launches himself at it, slamming it shut with all his body weight.*

> SHIT!

ALEX. Well exactly.

> *The locker rattles angrily.* BEN *is the only thing keeping* JIMMY *from hurtling out.*

> What are we going to do?

BEN. Go to my car, fetch the Taser!

ALEX. Good thinking!

> ALEX *runs off.*

BEN. We never had to wing it this much, not even at the bloody Giggle Factory!

JIMMY (*offstage.*) LET! ME! OUT!

> *The locker door crashes open, sending* BEN *tumbling stage-left.*

> Ben! You bastard. Think you could screw our comeback, did you? Who the hell do you think you are?

BEN, *wide-eyed in shock and panting heavily, looks at the sequinned blue hat and... has a dangerous idea: He puts the hat on, rearranges himself a little and then...*

BEN (*Sid impression*). Aye up, Jim. It's not Ben, it's me: Sid.

JIMMY *looks at him. The impression is very good, if a little nervous. Will this work...?* JIMMY *turns away.*

JIMMY.... Oh. Beg your pardon, Sid, thought you were that bastard Ben.

BEN *almost collapses in relief. Somehow, the ruse is working.*

BEN (*as Sid*). No, no. Not at all. Sid, I am. Yeah. Look at the hat: Sid.

JIMMY. Thought we were on red hats today?

BEN (*as Sid*). We were... but now... blue.

It's working, but BEN*'s still on thin ice.*

JIMMY. Listen! We've been sabotaged, lad! I knew Alex and Ben were hungry up-and-comers but I didn't think they'd go this far.

BEN (*as Sid*). Oh I know... bloody annoying, like... a Northern... problem.

JIMMY. What?

BEN (*as Sid*). Nothing. Nowt.

JIMMY. When I find that Ben... where did he go?

BEN (*as Sid*). Er... just... away... from here.

JIMMY. Onstage? Has the second act started!?

BEN (*as Sid*). No it hasn't, don't go onstage! No he went the other way... into the... basement.

JIMMY. Oh I see. You rumbled him so he hid like a rat, well he's gonna get it now, Sid!

JIMMY *exits.* BEN*'s got away with it! He discards his blue 'Sid' hat, then remembers:*

BEN (*alarmed*). Shit, the audience!

BEN *rushes out of the green room. The lighting switches to fully 'onstage' and* BEN *enters onto the stage.*

I am *so* sorry, ladies and gents! We'll be back on in one sec, thanks for your patience… (*Gets an idea.*) In the meantime, tell you what [GUEST*'s real name*], do you mind popping up and covering for a bit? Come on. If you're such a big deal, chance to redeem yourself.

The GUEST *is brought up onstage.*

Tell them about [*their famous work*] and your other little hobbies.

BEN *rushes off. The* GUEST *is left looking nervous and sheepish. The lighting becomes fully 'green room' and* BEN *enters backstage. He finds the* GUEST*, naturally, standing there.*

What are you doing? This is the backstage bit, yeah? Sit down!

BEN *sends the* GUEST *back to their seat.*

(*To himself.*) Okay, now where's Alex with that Taser…?

He looks off behind the curtain, stage-left, where he spots something aggravating 'onstage'.

Argh, what are they doing!?

He exits the green room, the lighting returning to fully 'onstage', then enters around the curtain. The GUEST *is, of course, no longer there.* BEN *confronts them in the audience.*

What are you doing? You're supposed to be covering for us? Run out of material already, have you? Come on!!

BEN *hauls the* GUEST *back onstage, then exits. The lighting goes fully 'green room'.* BEN *enters the green room.*

Okay well that buys me a bit more time – (*Sees the* GUEST *again.*) Are you joking? Right: you're a liability, I can't trust you, get in here.

BEN *ushers the* GUEST *into the stage-left locker, and shuts the door.* ALEX *runs on with the Taser.*

ALEX. Got the Taser!

ALEX *whips the stage-left locker door open in order to Taser* JIMMY, *but, of course, accidentally Tasers the* GUEST *as they emerge, baffled. The* GUEST *collapses back into the locker and* ALEX *slams the door shut.*

ALEX. Jimmy's changed!

BEN. Jimmy's in the basement.

ALEX. Oh right.

BEN. Gimme the Taser. I'll get Jimmy, you cover onstage!

BEN *takes the Taser and exits.*

ALEX. Alright, Benny!

Just as ALEX *turns to go back onstage,* SID *can be heard waking up in the kitchen, behind the curtain, stage-right.*

SID (*offstage*). Hello!?

ALEX *freezes on the spot. This too now!?*

Why was I in the kitchen?

SID *leaves the kitchen and enters the green room.*

SID / ALEX. Oh hello, Alex, lad. / Hello, Sid, you alright?

It's another awkward greeting, where neither knows who should speak first or if handshakes are happening or not. ALEX *takes his phone out and pulls his emergency parachute...*

ALEX. Yes, Mum, me again, any foreplay tips?

SID *walks stage-left to exit the green room.*

SID. Ah, I should get onstage anyway. We're doing the classics for Clint!

ALEX. Gonna call you back. (*Hangs up, then to* SID.) Don't go onstage!

SID. Why not?

ALEX *has to think on his feet.*

ALEX. It's still the interval and you're... *meant* to be in there.

ALEX *scrambles for something to say.*

Because, er, because... we're playing... Sardines!

SID. Sardines?

ALEX. As a warm-up! You know, the game where you hide and then you're joined by whoever finds you until there's only one person left looking?

SID. Ooh, sounds fun!

ALEX. Oh it genuinely is – and you found a hell of a hiding spot, Sid.

SID. Oh I best get back in then!

ALEX. *Exactly.* Stay hidden for a long time. *Perfect.*

ALEX*'s ploy has worked brilliantly. As* SID *goes to enter the kitchen,* ALEX *turns to exit for the stage.*

SID. You coming too?

ALEX (*turning back*). Huh?

SID. Well it's Sardines. You found me. You better get in too?

ALEX *realises the problem he's created.*

ALEX. Erm... well, *yes* but...

SID. Those are the rules, lad, come on!

ALEX (*gritted teeth*). Right... yeah... okay.

ALEX *has no choice but to follow* SID *into the kitchen.* BEN *runs back into the green room, and puts the Taser down.*

BEN. Can't find Jimmy anywhere. Alex, where are you?

JIMMY *enters.*

JIMMY. Can't find Ben anywhere. Sid, where are you?

BEN, *now on the other side of the stage from the Taser, but right next to* SID*'s blue hat, quickly yanks the hat back on just in time.*

BEN (*as Sid*). Yep, that's me, Sid, absolutely.

JIMMY. Well come on: we must have missed beginners' call cos they're waiting for us out there!

BEN (*as Sid*). Oh, er…

SID (*offstage, from the kitchen, gleeful, pre-recorded voice-over*). Oooh I think I can hear them!

BEN *realises that* SID *must have woken up.* JIMMY *turns towards the kitchen.*

JIMMY. What was that?

Now it's BEN*'s turn to scramble.*

BEN (*as Sid*)…. What was what?

JIMMY. Sounded like someone's in the kitchen?

BEN (*as Sid*). No.

JIMMY *turns to go.* BEN*'s in the clear. But then –*

SID (*offstage*). Think they're on to us!

JIMMY *turns towards the kitchen again.*

JIMMY. There it is again. Sounds like *you*, Sid!

BEN (*as Sid*). Yeah… that *was* me: I said 'think they're on to us', yeah… I just wanted to say that… yeah, I *do* think they're on to us.

JIMMY. Who?

BEN (*as Sid*)....The... RSPCA

JIMMY. What the hell are you talking about, come on, Sid, let's –

JIMMY turns to go.

SID (*offstage*). Ooh sorry is that your leg?

JIMMY turns back.

JIMMY. What?!

BEN has to keep this going...

BEN (*as Sid*). Is that your leg? Just... (*Points at* JIMMY*'s leg.*) Wondering if that... is indeed your leg?

JIMMY. My leg? What? Come on, we're going onstage!

JIMMY grabs BEN and hurls him out of the green room.

BEN (*as Sid*). Right, because I am Sid...

They exit. The lighting becomes fully 'onstage' and they both enter around the curtain, stage-right, with JIMMY *walking downstage to greet the audience and* BEN *lurking, terrified, by the curtain. Pretending to be* SID *backstage was one thing, but faking his way through a whole set?*

JIMMY. Hello, ladies and gentlemen, I am so sorry for the delay in starting the second act – come on, Sid, come here – but fear not, we're finally ready to go with an old favourite, 'The Mirror Routine'!

JIMMY gets into position far stage-right. BEN *obviously has no idea what to do, so just awkwardly stays centre-stage.*

(*Calling off.*) 'Alright, lads, I'm coming, just going to the bog, I'll be one sec.'

JIMMY turns, as in the sketch, but finds that BEN *has not moved. He's in completely the wrong place, smiling nervously at the audience.*

...What are you doing?! Get in position!

JIMMY *pretends to the audience that this is just* SID *messing about. He points stage-left and* BEN *repositions over there.*

BEN (*as Sid*). Right, yes, because I am Sid…

JIMMY. Okay, ladies and gents, from the top.

(*Calling off.*) 'Alright, lads, I'm coming, just going to the bog, I'll be one sec.'

JIMMY *walks into 'the bog', and turns to face* BEN. *But* JIMMY *sees that* BEN, *who has heard the word 'bog' and improvised as best he can, mimes flushing a toilet, then batting away the stench.*

BEN (*as Sid, riffing desperately*). 'Do not go in there.'

JIMMY. Sid – Mirror me! Like normal!

BEN (*as Sid*)…. Mirror you. Yep. Oh okay.

JIMMY. 'You ready for this, top fella?'

JIMMY *continues the actions of the sketch but, when it gets to the picking of something out of the teeth,* BEN *accidentally shoves his hand into* JIMMY*'s mouth.* JIMMY *recoils, aborts, and tries to save face.*

(*Frantically positive front.*) Okay, ha, there we go, the mirror sketch! (*Sotto to* SID.) Sid, are you okay, come on! (*To audience.*) Okay, let's get things *really* going with our classic song 'Peas in a Pod'! Maestro, please!

JIMMY *cues a musical backing track and takes out a microphone.*

(*Sings.*)
'I'm Jim and I'm a ladies' man
With jokes that you'll adore
This lad right here's my biggest fan
I'll let him tell you more.'

He passes the microphone to BEN, *who does the best he can…*

BEN (*as Sid*)....I'm Sid and... yeah... that's genuinely... me. Er... yeah... I'm Sid.

JIMMY *looks confused and takes the mic back.*

JIMMY. Er, okay, let's move on instead, ladies and gents, to 'The Comedy Count'!

JIMMY *cues new music, which provides a throbbing fairground rhythm. The lyrics come thick and fast.*

'One, two, three, four
We've got japes and pranks galore!'

He passes the mic to BEN, *who thinks on his feet.*

BEN (*as Sid*). Five, six, seven, eight, you... alright, mate?

JIMMY*'s perplexed at this, and takes back the mic.*

JIMMY. 'Nine, ten, eleven, twelve
Into bits and skits we'll delve!'

Mic to BEN.

BEN (*as Sid*). Thirteen, fourteen, fifteen, sixteen, those... are the numbers from... thirteen to sixteen.

Mic to a fuming JIMMY.

JIMMY. 'Seventeen, eighteen, nineteen, twenty
Songs and ditties we've got plenty!'

Mic to BEN, *who's properly running out of steam now.*

BEN (*as Sid*). Twenty-one, twenty-two, twenty-three, twenty-four, that's... Christmas Eve so make sure, be certain to have a... you know... a great Christmas when that comes around.

JIMMY *indicates for the music to cut.* BEN *fumbles on desperately.*

And if you haven't got those to celebrate with or who... will support you and your interests then... well... find people who you can chat to, or write to, cos online friendships are popular now, aren't they, so... act accordingly to give yourself, er... yeah, the best possible chance for a good time, all the time. Travel abroad maybe if –

JIMMY *aborts the whole thing and hauls* BEN *up towards the curtain.*

JIMMY. One moment, ladies and gents, Sid's not feeling too well so we just need to pop backstage and then we'll be with you again in a moment.

They exit around the curtain. The lighting returns to fully 'green room' and they enter.

What were you doing out there!?

BEN (*as Sid*). Er... yeah, sorry –

JIMMY. You were the one who wanted to do the old favourites, then you completely let us down. You stay here, Sid, I've got to go and salvage something.

JIMMY, *genuinely disappointed in his old mucker, exits.* BEN, *a bit shaken, removes the 'Sid' hat and breathes heavily.* ALEX *emerges from the kitchen.*

ALEX (*to kitchen*). You stay here, Sid. I've got to go and check something...

He rushes over to BEN.

(*Sotto.*) Ben! How did it go, did you get Jimmy?

BEN. No, he caught me, so I had to think on my feet.

ALEX. Why have you got Sid's hat?

BEN. I've been pretending to *be* Sid.

ALEX. Oh God. Nice one! Didn't know you were such a master of disguise!

ALEX *takes the hat from* BEN's *hands and toys with it.*

BEN. Well, you learn a few things when you're part of the Ultimate Protection Squad.

ALEX.... UPS?

BEN. Ultimate Protection –

ALEX. Squad, sure.

BEN. Why were you in the kitchen?

ALEX. Sid woke up too, but don't worry, I've handled it. So, wait, where's Jimmy now?

BEN. Onstage.

ALEX. Oh my God.

BEN. Don't worry...

> BEN *grabs the mouth gag, the other blue hat, and the net.*

> This'll sort him out.

ALEX. Tidy his hair?

BEN. Net him!

ALEX. When it returns fully sized, yep.

BEN. Keep Sid in here.

ALEX. Okay. Ooh, *I* could pretend to be *Jimmy*?!

BEN. Whatever – just don't let him out.

> BEN *exits.* ALEX *puts the blue hat on and tries his* JIMMY *impression out with a cheeky grin. It's passable but over-the-top.*

ALEX. 'Ooh, I'm Jimmy, and Sid: you need to stop messing around!'

> SID *emerges from the kitchen.*

SID. Alright, Jim, it was just a game of Sardines. Shall we go onstage then?

> SID, *clearly, thinks that* ALEX *is* JIMMY. ALEX *decides in the moment he has to go ahead with it.*

ALEX (*as Jimmy*). No way.

SID. Why not?

ALEX (*as Jimmy*). Because... we need to have a chat.

SID. Oh, okay...

ALEX (*as Jimmy*). Sid, I've got something very serious to tell you.

ALEX *blocks the exit and gestures for* SID *to sit.* SID*'s worried.*

SID. Oh my God, what on earth are you gonna say?

ALEX (*as Jimmy*). Er, every weekend, Sid, I... and I feel you should know this... I pay someone... to cover me... in... jam.

SID *stares at him.*

SID (*I know*). Yeah: Richard... your jam-spreader.

ALEX (*as Jimmy, gobsmacked but having to roll with it*). Er... oh. Right, yeah.

SID. Is that it? You bringing up your jam-spreader I already know about? Now come on!

SID *drags* ALEX *towards the exit.* ALEX *scrambles into fifth gear.*

ALEX (*as Jimmy*). WAIT!!

SID. What now?!

ALEX (*as Jimmy*). I NEED TO GIVE YOU A SPECIAL TREAT!!

SID. Oh really?

ALEX (*as Jimmy*). YEAH. THAT'S WHAT THIS HAS ALL BEEN ABOUT!

SID (*softening*). Okay, well what is it?

ALEX (*as Jimmy*). I NEED TO BRING IT IN SO YOU GET IN THE KITCHEN AND THEN IT'LL BE A NICE SURPRISE OKAY?

SID. Okay! Oh I *love* this!

SID *gets back in the kitchen.* ALEX *looks desperately for something that could constitute a present. There's nothing! He has a brainwave. He opens the stage-left locker and brings out the frazzled* GUEST.

ALEX. Right, chance to redeem yourself. There's an old bloke in there who might come out any second. I need to make sure Ben's okay, so you're just gonna stand here and greet him when he comes out and say, 'Hello I'm your special treat', and keep him here, okay?

The GUEST *weakly protests.*

JUST DO IT.

ALEX *hangs his blue hat on the hatstand and exits. The* GUEST *stands there, baffled. After a beat,* BEN, *still wearing his blue hat, enters, marching* JIMMY *in, who is gagged and tangled in the net.*

BEN (*calling round the curtain*). Alex, buy us some time. I'll be there in a sec.

BEN *sits the netted* JIMMY *on the chair. He is about to go back onstage but notices the* GUEST *standing in the middle of the room!*

What are you *doing*!? It's all about you, isn't it? Get back in there.

BEN *points at the locker. The* GUEST, *completely resigned now, climbs back into it.* BEN *shuts the door and turns to the tied-up* JIMMY, *who watches on, flabbergasted at the revelation that this wasn't actually* SID *at all, but* BEN. BEN *performatively takes off the blue hat and discards it.*

Oh, yeah: sorry I messed up your 'Mirror Routine'.

JIMMY *struggles furiously to escape but can't, and* BEN *exits.* SID *steps out from the kitchen.*

SID. Alright then, Jim, what's my surprise treat?!

He sees the netted, gagged JIMMY. *This, he thinks, must be the 'treat'.*

…Oh. Okay! You've put yourself into a net… Right. Why not? I love that Jim. 'You in a net', very clever.

JIMMY *is trying to scream at him through the gag*.

What? What are you saying, Jim?

SID *takes the gag off* JIMMY.

JIMMY. You half-brain! We've been sabotaged!!!

SID.…is this part of the treat?

JIMMY. I'll treat you to a bruised ear unless you get me out of this net!

SID. '*Out* of the net', why'd you put yourself in it then?

JIMMY. Ben put me in it! He's been pretending to be you! Came onstage and all, *ruined* 'Peas in a Pod'.

SID *is struggling to take all this in*.

SID.…So there *isn't* a treat?

JIMMY. Why d'you keep banging on about treats?!

SID. Just now, you said, 'Get in the kitchen, I'll bring you your treat.'

JIMMY. I never said anything of the – Oooh! Okay, so *Alex* has been pretending to be *me* as well.

SID. So that was *Alex*!?

JIMMY. Yes!

SID. And *Ben's* been acting as me!?

JIMMY. Yes!

SID. And that explains *Sardines*!?

JIMMY. Ye– 'Sardines'!? I can't help you with that – Get me out of this!

SID *helps* JIMMY *out of the net*.

SID. But, Jim, why would they do all this!?

JIMMY. To steal our comeback! So come on, let's sort those
bastards out!

JIMMY *and* SID *exit.*

*Dramatic music, as an old-school Warner Bros-style chase
sequence begins.* BEN *runs on, chased by* JIMMY, *who now
brandishes the whisky bottle.*

BEN. Whoa, Jimmy, calm down, mate, calm down!

JIMMY. Get back here, Ben, get back here, you bastard!

BEN *runs into the kitchen, followed by* JIMMY, *who
immediately exits the kitchen, now pursued by* BEN, *who
brandishes the darts-sharpening knife.*

Put that down, Ben. Calm down now, mate. Don't be hasty,
lad.

BEN. Come on then!

JIMMY *exits the green room chased by* BEN. JIMMY
immediately re-enters, pursued by SID *carrying the net.*

JIMMY. Sid, why are *you* chasing me?

SID. I dunno, I'm awful confused!

JIMMY *exits.* ALEX *enters.*

ALEX. Ben? Benny?

SID *turns.*

Oh, *Sid*?

SID. Hello, Alex.

*The chase music cuts and their awkward greetings reach a
new height, with* SID *offering* ALEX *a handshake whilst
holding the net, resulting in* ALEX *getting tangled in the net
and* SID *then throwing the rest of the net over him.*

Alright then, Alex, have a good chase!

ALEX. Okay thanks, Sid, bye, mate!

They exit in opposite directions.

JIMMY *enters, running away from* BEN, *who pursues him with the javelin.*

JIMMY *exits round the curtain stage-left, and enters 'onstage'. The lighting splits.* BEN *remains backstage by the stage-left curtain.*

JIMMY. I really am *so sorry*, ladies and gents.

BEN *lunges at him with the javelin from backstage, and it 'reappears' beside* JIMMY *as a small javelin.* JIMMY *takes it gratefully, and uses it to help emphasise his points.*

We've got a few teething problems, we'll be just a moment.

BEN *reaches behind the curtain, grabbing* JIMMY*'s leg, and pulling it back towards him (this is, of course, in fact the* JIMMY DOUBLE*'s leg). Simultaneously the* SID DOUBLE*'s hand reaches out onstage and grabs* JIMMY*'s leg.*

It's really nothing to worry about.

JIMMY *clatters to the floor and is dragged offstage.*

And I can assure you that it'll be worth the wait!!

BEN *pulls the* JIMMY DOUBLE *from behind the stage-left curtain and off into the wings.*

A model of the set is wheeled on with four puppets representing ALEX, BEN, JIMMY *and* SID. *All lights cut except a spotlight downstage-centre, and the chase sequence is now presented as a puppet show. After a few moments the music cuts and* BEN *puts his head round the corner.*

BEN. What the hell are you doing?

ALEX *reveals himself behind the model of the set. This has all been his whimsical idea.*

ALEX. Oh, sorry.

BEN. We're in the middle of a chase! Don't start messing about with puppets!

ALEX. No sure, helluva point.

BEN exits. ALEX follows after him, with his model and puppets.

BEN re-enters, looking over his shoulder, having temporarily escaped JIMMY.

JIMMY (*offstage*). Ben? Where are you!? I'm coming for you, boy! Benjamin? Ben?

BEN looks around frantically for a good hiding place.

Bennnnnnnnn!

BEN desperately grabs an empty picture frame and a baseball cap. He puts the cap on, holds the frame up to his face, and freezes his expression to make it look like he is a painting. The music cuts as JIMMY bounds in. He peers around the room suspiciously.

Hmmm... no sign of him.

JIMMY *spots 'the painting'.*

Ah! Someone's finally hung up my portrait of a baseballer! (*Looks away, satisfied.*) ...Waittasecond! I don't have a portrait of a baseballer!...

BEN's eyes widen in fear.

I have a portrait of a skateboarder!

BEN twists his hat so it's back-to-front. JIMMY turns to inspect the painting. He's happy that it's as he remembers.

Mm, mm! (*Looks away, satisfied.*) ...Waittasecond! My portrait of a skateboarder doesn't have a frame!

BEN takes the frame away from his face. JIMMY turns.

Mm, mm! (*Looks away, satisfied.*) ...Waittasecond! The golf club isn't *open* on a Wednesday. My wife *is* having an affair!!

BEN goes to do something, but realises he doesn't have to as, bizarrely, this is a separate point.

Waittasecond! The skateboarder in my portrait is [*ethnicity that the actor playing* SID/BEN *is not*].

JIMMY turns. BEN is frozen. Surely he's not going to try and adopt another ethnicity…

BEN…. yeah, I'm not gonna do that.

BEN exits.

JIMMY. *Ben!?* Ben, you bastard!!!!

Before JIMMY *can follow* BEN, *SID enters.*

SID. They're too quick, Jim, it's no use.

JIMMY. We need them out the building, let's *scare them off*!

JIMMY grabs the Frankenstein's monster and mouse masks.

We put these on, hide, and leap out.

SID. Oh very good, Jim! From the locker?

SID moves toward the stage-left locker.

JIMMY. Yeah – no, wait!

JIMMY moves to the stage-right locker (the one with the 'out of order' sign on it).

Let's do it from *this* locker, that'll proper shock 'em!

SID puts on the Frankenstein's monster mask. JIMMY *puts the mouse mask on, and opens the stage-right locker door.*

SID. Oooh, like a game of Sardines!

JIMMY. Can you stop bringing up Sardines?

JIMMY walks into the locker. Somehow, however, he immediately reappears through the stage-left locker as if he has teleported across the stage! (This is actually, of course, the JIMMY DOUBLE *wearing the same mask and red hat.*)

SID. Whoa, Jim! How'd you get over there?

JIMMY DOUBLE shrugs in confusion and gets back into the stage-left locker. JIMMY *immediately re-enters through the stage-right locker.*

JIMMY. That's dead weird.

SID *experiments by poking his arm through the stage-right locker. Immediately the arm sticks out through the stage-left locker. (Again, of course, the* SID DOUBLE.)

SID. Here, Jim, look behind you!

JIMMY *turns to face the stage-left locker and sees* SID *giving him the finger.*

JIMMY. You cheeky bastard!

JIMMY *turns to face* SID *again to find that* SID *has pulled his mask down to give him a fright.*

Ooh, just get in the locker, Sid!

From this point onwards, the action speeds up into a relentless flurry of movement: JIMMY *shoves* SID *into the stage-right locker and immediately* SID DOUBLE *stumbles out through the stage-left locker.* JIMMY *continues to look through the stage-right locker.*

Sid. Sid? Where are you, lad?

SID DOUBLE *rushes up behind him.* JIMMY *turns.*

Oh there you are! Come on, Sid. We need to *hide*!

They both enter the stage-right locker. The JIMMY DOUBLE *and* SID *appear through the stage-left locker.*

SID. That locker's no good, let's just hide in the kitchen.

They go into the kitchen. Instantly, JIMMY *and the* SID DOUBLE *appear from the exit previously used for 'the basement'.*

JIMMY. The kitchen's no good! Let's try *this* locker!

JIMMY *gestures for the* SID DOUBLE *to go into the stage-left locker. Once he has done so,* SID *appears through the stage-right locker.*

SID. That locker's no good neither.

JIMMY. Hm – let's try this locker again.

JIMMY *ushers* SID *into the stage-right locker. The* SID DOUBLE *appears through the stage-left locker.*

Try it again, Sid.

The SID DOUBLE *carries on walking, and enters the stage-right locker. A* SECOND SID DOUBLE *appears through the stage-left locker.*

Try it again, Sid.

The SECOND SID DOUBLE *carries on walking, and enters the stage-right locker.* SID *appears through the stage-left locker.*

SID. I'm not sure this is working.

JIMMY. Give it another go, Sid.

SID *carries on walking, and enters the stage-right locker. The* SID DOUBLE *appears through the stage-left locker.*

Give it one more go, Sid.

The SID DOUBLE *carries on walking, and enters the stage-right locker. The* SECOND SID DOUBLE *appears through the stage-left locker.*

Try it again, Sid.

The SECOND SID DOUBLE *carries on walking, and enters the stage-right locker.* SID *appears through the stage-left locker.*

SID. You *sure* this is –

JIMMY. One final try!

SID *carries on walking, and enters the stage-right locker. The* SID DOUBLE *appears through the stage-left locker.*

I've got a good feeling about this one!

The SID DOUBLE *walks towards the stage-right locker, but before he reaches it,* BEN *storms in from the basement, holding the net.*

BEN. Got you now, Jimmy!

The SID DOUBLE *scarpers into the kitchen.* BEN *bears down on* JIMMY, *so* JIMMY *jumps into the stage-left locker.* JIMMY DOUBLE *immediately re-enters through the stage-right locker.* BEN *is baffled.*

What the...?

BEN *chases across to stage-right but* JIMMY DOUBLE *jumps through the stage-right locker and reappears through the stage-left one before* BEN *can get to him.* BEN *goes across to nab him stage-left, but again* JIMMY *jumps through the stage-left locker and the* JIMMY DOUBLE *reappears through the stage-right one.* BEN *chases him once more, but as the* JIMMY DOUBLE *approaches the stage-right locker, this time* BEN *pre-empts the magic and smugly prepares the net by the stage-left locker. When the* JIMMY DOUBLE *does disappear through the stage-right locker, however, it's not* JIMMY *who appears from the stage-left locker, but the* GUEST.

You! *Again!?!*

BEN *furiously ushers them back into the stage-left locker.* ALEX *enters.*

ALEX. Where are they, Benny?

JIMMY DOUBLE *and* SID DOUBLE *enter from the basement holding, respectively, the baking tray and Taser gun.*

ALEX *and* BEN, *rabbits in the headlights, run for the stage-right and stage-left lockers respectively.* JIMMY DOUBLE *follows* ALEX, *and* SID DOUBLE *follows* BEN. *As they reach the locker entrances they turn back to each other and give a thumbs-up, then dive into the lockers simultaneously, slamming the doors behind them.*

The lockers shake violently for a moment, then the stage-left one bursts open and BEN *stumbles out holding his jaw, followed by the* SID DOUBLE *doing the same, followed by the life-size Action Man. What!? The* SID DOUBLE *tackles the doll back into the locker, followed by* BEN, *who slams the door behind him.*

Immediately, the stage-right locker opens and ALEX *leans out, a hand strangling his neck. He steps out into view to reveal that he's just accidentally strangling himself. He re-enters the locker and slams the door behind him. The stage-left locker swings open and* SID DOUBLE *emerges, holding the Taser. He turns back and jams the Taser into the locker.* BEN's *arms and legs flail wildly into view, electrified.* SID *jumps back in and slams the door behind him.*

The stage-right locker opens and JIMMY DOUBLE *jumps out with the baking tray. As* ALEX *emerges,* JIMMY DOUBLE *smashes the tray into his head and* ALEX *stumbles back in, followed by* JIMMY DOUBLE, *who closes the door behind him.* SID *and* JIMMY *enter from the stage-left and stage-right lockers simultaneously, and take off their masks, and put their red hats back on. The music fades away; the dramatic chase is over.*

SID. Well done, Jim.

JIMMY. Okay, we'll deal with them later, but for now we just get back onstage and –

The sound of a powerful car revving up and pulling away. Clint's? They stop in their tracks and listen as it fades. SID *steps onto the stool and looks through the window.*

SID. Yeah. He's gone.

It's over. All of it. Their hopes, their golden chance... gone. JIMMY *helps* SID *off the chair.*

JIMMY. Right.

SID. So... so that's that then.

JIMMY spots their old programme, takes it off the noticeboard, and sits.

JIMMY. Yeah. Let's be honest, Sid, with the second act they've had, the whole audience will have packed up and gone.

SID. Can't really blame them.

JIMMY. A bungled 'Peas in a Pod' with an imposter, and then an empty stage for twenty minutes. No, not exactly the old killer act.

SID. Even worse than Minsk.

SID has tried to make JIMMY laugh, but JIMMY remains silent. SID tries a different tack.

Well... I guess we just do the classics properly tomorrow, build the comeback from there.

JIMMY. There's no comeback without Clint.

JIMMY's not got the energy for this any more. It's time to make SID accept reality.

SID. There... there might be another... Hollywood director in another... town –

JIMMY. Come on, Sid. That was our one chance to get out of Didlington and make people...

He's not sure if he can say it as nakedly as this, but he does.

...and make people love us again. Let's just pack up now and we can decide about the rest of the tour tomorrow.

SID accepts it's over. He mournfully picks up his jacket and goes to put it away. JIMMY holds out the old programme to be packed away too. SID, pained, takes it and goes to leave. As he's about to disappear behind the curtain, he stops. He's seen something.

SID. Jim?

JIMMY. I know it's all booked but –

SID. Jim?

JIMMY. I don't want to talk about it now, Sid –

SID. Jimmy?

JIMMY. What?

SID (*disbelief and joy*). They're still here!

JIMMY.... Who?

SID. The audience, they're all... sat there.

JIMMY. Don't wind me up.

SID. I'm not!

JIMMY. Why on earth would they – after the filth they've been served up?

SID. Come and look.

JIMMY joins SID by the curtain.

JIMMY.... Even the pizza guy!

They gaze behind the curtain for a moment in silence.

They're waiting... for *us*.

The implications of this wash over them.

We better get back out there!

They burst into action to get their costumes back on.

SID. Oh my God. Do the old act!

JIMMY. Give the real Jimmy and Sid to the real fans!

They help each other into their jackets.

SID. Bloody hell, I know it's not millions watching on TV again, but I guess –

JIMMY. Guess they must love us. King-makers of Didlington after all.

SID. So... so, the tour goes on?

JIMMY. I think it has to, Sid! Until one of us collapses.

SID. Ha. An 'open-ended' tour?

JIMMY (*enjoying the phrase*). We dish out the old act until we're literally too old to act.

They're closer and more energised than ever.

SID. Hah, yeah! Until we can't get through 'Mirror' cos your knees have gone.

JIMMY. Ha, and yours. (*Beat.*) Although actually –

SID. That'd work quite well –

SID / JIMMY. If it was both of us, yeah. / It'd be mirrored.

They smile.

SID. Are we seriously talking about this? Our 'farewell' tour?

JIMMY gestures for SID to lead on, then, just before SID exits around the curtain to go onstage, JIMMY puts a hand on his shoulder.

We've got each other. I think we can handle the end.

They exit the green room, round the curtain stage-left, as if to go onstage. ALEX and BEN stumble out of the stage-right and stage-left lockers respectively.

BEN. Where are they?

ALEX. Wait, wait! They've gone.

BEN. Oh no…

BEN runs to turn on the Tannoy. His worst fears are confirmed: it's JIMMY and SID onstage.

JIMMY (*voice-over*). Thank you, thank you! Well, ladies and gentlemen, sorry for putting you through all that tonight, thanks for sticking around.

SID (*voice-over*). We're going to bring things to a close with an old favourite.

JIMMY (*voice-over*). Done properly, this time. Maestro, please!

Musical backing starts up. ALEX and BEN are now watching on from behind the curtain, as they were at the beginning of Act One, Scene Two.

(*Sings*.) 'I'm Jim and I'm a ladies' man
with jokes that you'll adore
This lad right here's my biggest fan
I'll let him tell you more.'

SID (*sings, voice-over*).
'I'm Sid I'm simple and aware
It's daft to be with him
But here is why we are a pair
Now where shall we begin...'

JIMMY *and* SID (*singing, voice-over*).
'When you're lonely and low
You've got nowhere you can go
Look for someone who makes life glow
Find them then you're not on your tod
You'll be two peas – '

BEN *stops watching, and turns off the Tannoy. A grim pause. He sits.*

ALEX. So... so that's that, then.

BEN....yeah.

ALEX. What a mad one.

They've blown it. Royally. But then... BEN *breaks into laughter.*

BEN. You'd be hard pressed to accuse us of not winging it! I knew we were screwed when we couldn't even get Sherlock's chair right.

ALEX. Oh, I was losing my mind!

BEN. No you did well covering that bit, when you said 'that's *exactly* how it's written'.

ALEX. Well I was like: got to say something!

BEN. And what the hell happened with the Sherlock song?

ALEX. Yeah the audience got it right first time!

BEN. So weird! Haha, God, I can't tell you how bad I was at 'Peas in a Pot.'

ALEX. 'Pod.'

BEN. Right, well yeah, exactly.

ALEX.... man. So, it's over. We go our separate ways.

BEN. Yeah. Well unless we went cap in hand back to the bloody Giggle Factory.

ALEX. Hah, yeah imagine!

They laugh. Haunting music fades in gently. BEN *looks at* ALEX.

BEN. I mean... we could?

ALEX. Really? Back to The Giggle Factory?

BEN *gets up. His body feels lighter. His mind clearer.*

BEN. *They'd* still have us.

ALEX. Right... so we'd just be like, 'Ladies and gents, thanks for having us back, first up, "The Ghost Swimming Teacher"'?

BEN. Well ideally you wouldn't say *that*.

ALEX. Oh sorry... 'The Ghost Swimming *Instructor*'?

BEN *isn't bothered any more by the sloppiness. In fact, he loves it. He sizes his friend up: this is the man he's bound to. Kindness comes easily.*

BEN.... sure.

ALEX. Are we seriously talking about this? Back to the beginning?

BEN. We've got each other, I think we can handle starting again. (*Looking at* ALEX*'s sweaty face.*) Do you need a towel?

ALEX. Oh yeah, thanks.

BEN passes ALEX a towel. ALEX mops his face. Then BEN gets two beers out and passes one to ALEX. They open and cheers each other.

Then, in unspoken agreement, they bust out their secret handshake.

SLAM!!! Suddenly, the stalls door in the auditorium swings open. ALEX and BEN, startled, look over.

An OLD MAN stands in the doorway. He looks like a Victorian vaudevillian, in a battered tailcoat and spongebag trousers.

Slowly, he glides over to the stage and steps up onto it. As the music swells, he approaches ALEX and BEN. They seem nervous, but prepared, as if soldiers on parade.

The OLD MAN reaches into his pocket and pulls out a bunch of grapes. With precise movements he approaches ALEX and feeds him a grape. As ALEX chews, the OLD MAN offers a ceremonial nod, which ALEX returns. He then approaches BEN and does the same, before he goes back towards the auditorium exit, turning one final time to offer a proud, congratulatory nod.

As the OLD MAN in the tailcoat disappears beyond the doorway, ALEX and BEN turn to look at each other. They smile, and hug.

Blackout.

The End.

www.nickhernbooks.co.uk

facebook.com/nickhernbooks

twitter.com/nickhernbooks